*Dedicated to all who honor the flag
by upholding the ideals of the Constitution.*

Currier & Ives, 1860 – 1880 (ZFC0315)

…This flag which we honor and under which we serve

is the emblem of our unity, our power,

our thought and purpose as a nation.

It has no other character than that

which we give it from generation to generation.

The choices are ours.

Woodrow Wilson, June 14, 1917

The American Flag
Two Centuries of Concord & Conflict

Howard Michael Madaus & Whitney Smith
Introduction by Wayne Fields

VZ PUBLICATIONS
Santa Cruz, California

Acknowledgements

The American Flag: Two Centuries of Concord & Conflict, from the collections of Ben Zaricor, Louise Veninga, and Kit Hinrichs, was first exhibited in 2003 at the Presidio of San Francisco, California. The exhibition was sponsored by Good Earth® Teas, Pentagram, and The Presidio Trust of San Francisco.

We would like to thank the following persons for their participation in the exhibition and book:

Howard Michael Madaus, *Curator*

Whitney Smith, *Vexillologist*

Pat Warfield, *Framing and Display*

Fonda Thomsen, *Textile Preservationist*

John Thompson, *Exhibit Director*

John Amaro, *Exhibit Manager*

Kit Hinrichs, *Creative Director*

Roberto Avila, *Book Design*

Myrna Newcomb, *Design*

Douglas Sandberg, *Photography*

James Ferrigan, *Technical Advisor and Editing*

Tim Hill, *Production Coordinator*

Louise Veninga, *Co-Publisher*

Ben Zaricor, *Co-Publisher, Editor*

Significant contributions were also made by Philip Koch, Michael Semler, MacKenzie Communications, Sterling Rana Group, Melanie Clark, Martha Diaz, Piero Milani and Terry Heffernan.

ISBN 0-97551-680-9 (hardcover), 0-97551-681-7 (softcover). © 2006 by Veninga-Zaricor Publications, Publisher, info@vzpublications.com, c/o The Flag Center, 849C Almar Ave. Box 155, Santa Cruz, CA 95060, info@flagcenter.org. All rights reserved. Coordinated by Artbook Press, P.O. Box 6, Sinclair, ME 04779-0006. Assistance in text and research was provided by the Flag Research Center, Box 580, Winchester, MA 01890-0880. Produced in the United States of America and printed in Hong Kong. No part of this book may be reproduced without permission in writing from the publisher. First Printing.

Supported by the Veninga-Zaricor family, The Flag Center and Good Earth® Teas of Santa Cruz, California.

Contents

INTRODUCTION
Indivisible, *Page 6*
By Wayne Fields

 GALLERY I

A New Constellation: 13 Stars and 13 Stripes for a New Nation, *Page 8*
The Flag Resolution of 1777

 GALLERY II

A New Star for Every State, *Page 30*
The Flag Act of 1794

 GALLERY III

The End of Compromise: Stars Excluded, Stars Defended, *Page 52*
"Exclusionary Flags," 1850–1860

 GALLERY IV

"Guide on the Colors!," *Page 68*
American Flags in Conflict

 GALLERY V

Manifest Destiny: New Stars for a New Land, *Page 92*
The Centennial Celebration

 GALLERY VI

A Symbol of World Power: the Stars & Stripes at Home and Abroad, *Page 112*
An Equal Among the World's Powers

EPILOGUE
Patriotism and War, *Page 140*
By Henry Berger

THOUGHTS OF A COLLECTOR
Whose Flag Is It, Anyway? *Page 142*
By Ben Reed Zaricor

Abraham Lincoln Funeral Flag, *Page 143*

Stripes, Stars and States, *Page 144*

Index, *Page 146*

Glossary, *Page 148*

INTRODUCTION

Indivisible

A speech given at the opening of the exhibit The American Flag: Two Centuries of Concord & Conflict, *at the Presidio's Officers Club in San Francisco, California, January 12, 2003.*

Introduction by Wayne Fields

*13-Star U.S. Flag,
About 1845 – 1850*

The founding fathers defined one of the most complicated plot lines that was ever assigned to a people to enact and to explore, and they did it in ways which I don't think they fully understood or to some extent ever hoped would work out successfully. They had a kind of simple but contradictory commitment that a people could somehow be both one and many. We carry that motto around on our coins—so convinced are we of its sacred nature—that says we are, somehow simultaneously, *plura* and *unum*.

The founders were not calling on us, as the leaders of other nations had, to become one from what had been many or to break apart and become many from what had been one. The plot line they designed was one in which we would be one and many *at the same time*. That we would somehow be able, as the Declaration of Independence insists, to define ourselves out of a fiercely suspicious nature built around our notion that individual rights take the highest priority and our commitment to affection as made in the opening line of the Constitution that *we the people*—and not the states, as the Confederation had imagined it—*we the people* are committed to a more perfect union.

The tension between those two parts of our heritage is acted out in the flag. The story that we see in the stripes and the stars is about the aspiration (and, often enough, about our failure to obtain it), to somehow carry that story forward into the demands of our own time. No design firm in America would come up with this flag. You can hear the criticisms—It's much too busy. Rectangles inside rectangles?—I don't think so! Stars next to stripes? And those colors! The busyness of it is because it is trying to retain the multiplicity of America in a single symbol. The fact that it has constantly been changing on us, reforming itself with the addition of states, and (I would argue) that through those same statements of transformation, changing in terms of the addition of cultures, addition of rights, addition of understanding of one another. All this has been extraordinary testimony to the persistence of an idea that, according to conventional wisdom, now as much as in the time of the founders, simply will not work.

As we see more and more how the new republics that were formed after the fall of the Soviet Union become increasingly convinced that only communities of likeness can be one, that only communities in which difference has been eliminated can be successful as communities, we begin to understand the depth of the importance of our struggle with this story line and also the extraordinary commitment it has taken to carry it this far and to move it ahead.

I will skip any elaboration of that beyond saying that the place where I find it most interestingly expressed was in the recent exposure that we've had in the excitement of flags in the aftermath of 9/11 when they were flying everywhere and commentary was being written about that display of patriotism in every major city of the United States.

I was not in a major city most of that time. I was traveling around a part of rural Missouri and southern Iowa where very few people or media and politicians go by the farms. Very few of those farms are prospering now, yet a group of people that has become as impoverished and as marginalized as many people in our inner cities had flags flying there for nobody in particular to see, since nobody in particular ever drove by those farms.

One of them happened to be the farm of an acquaintance of mine. I asked him—a very crotchety man who makes me look pleasant by contrast—why he had done this, since he literally lives on a road that nobody else takes. What he tried to explain was that for him it wasn't a sign of defiance. He didn't expect any Al-Qaeda to suddenly jump up in a soybean field. It was the only way he had of showing solidarity with the people that he had never seen before but considered his countrymen. He has never been to New York, has no aspiration to go to New York, and wouldn't care much for New York if he ever got there. But New Yorkers were for him, like the rest of his more immediate dysfunctional family, people that were to be cared for and loved in spite of himself and in spite of themselves.

The flag has become not something we just say to the rest of the world. The flag is something we say to one another—and in my friend's case, to himself—about the deepest and profoundest commitments that make us a people. We understand that the symbol of our unity is also the symbol of our exclusion in crucial moments. It is tremendously important to go back and look at photographs of domestic strife, domestic demonstrations in every generation, to see that the flag is always there. That the suffragettes are waving it at the beginning of the century, that it leads the demonstrations at Selma and at Montgomery, that there is a constant effort to claim it in its fullest and most inclusive terms by people who have often been excluded in every other statement of who we are.

For me the great loss—and I have a jaundiced view of this because when "one nation under God" was added I had been saying the Pledge of Allegiance in school for about ten years already and had to learn it again or look like an idiot every time if I did not put in "under God"—was this: as important as that phrase was which the Baptist minister who wrote the original Pledge of Allegiance did not see the need for, the word it shouldered aside was *indivisible.*

Whatever God has to do with us and thinks of us, our security and real strength is only as great as our commitment to one another, and only so much as we believe that in some important way these diverse people that we have come to live among are people who can make us feel more secure and more at home than people who might be precisely like us. We are *indivisible* and we *are* indivisible because of a commitment to law and to justice and to each other.

This to me is the national story that the founders began to write but of course never imagined anybody finishing, at least not with a happy ending. This is the story that the flag contains in some important way. It is the story whose latest chapter depends upon what we write and whether we find it possible to write it together or whether we finally despair and let the story end.

Wayne Fields, the Lynne Cooper Harvey Distinguished Chair in English and Director of American Culture Studies at Washington University in St. Louis, Missouri, received his doctorate from the University of Chicago. His articles on subjects ranging from contemporary politics to the American prairie have appeared in such periodicals as American Heritage. *He is the author of three books,* Union of Words: A History of Presidential Eloquence, The Past Leads a Life of Its Own, *and* What the River Knows: An Angler in Mid-Stream.

GALLERY I

A New Constellation: 13 Stars and 13 Stripes for a New Nation

The Flag Resolution of 1777

"Resolved, that the Flag of the united states be 13 stripes alternate red and white, that the Union be 13 stars white in a blue field representing a new constellation."
— *Journal of the Continental Congress*

On June 14, 1777, barely three weeks shy of the first anniversary of the signing of the Declaration of Independence, the Second Continental Congress finally adopted a resolution formalizing the young nation's new flag—the "Stars & Stripes." Juxtapositioned with other resolutions concerning naval affairs, the simple resolve delineated the basic design of the flag, but at the same time it ignored many details: Were the stripes to be horizontal or vertical? Would a red or a white stripe begin the alternating sequence? How were the stars to be arranged in this blue union? What were to be the proportions or relative size of this union? And, how many points would each star have? Were these details even considered important?

Fortuitously, several of these issues had already been resolved in the making of the previous flag that had represented the Congress—the "Grand Union" or "Continental" Flag. Already resolved was the question of the direction of the stripes—they had been horizontal—and the red stripe usually took precedence (although every now and then a flag might start with white!). The main issue left unresolved concerned the blue union and its thirteen white stars. And that issue would remain unresolved for 135 years. But those vagaries presented the American people with the latitude in the design and manufacture of the flag that opened a span of "folk art" that has only recently been fully appreciated.

The Forster Flag; First Essex County Militia Regiment, Manchester Company Color (Massachusetts-Bay) from the Revolutionary War

Date:
About 1774; modified 1775/1776

Size:
58.5" hoist x 63" fly

Medium:
Hand-sewn silk

Provenance:
Acquired by the Flag Heritage Foundation (Winchester, Mass.) in 1975 from the heirs of the original color-bearer.

This is the oldest surviving flag featuring 13 stripes honoring the original 13 colonies. The obverse side shown above has six white stripes against a red background, while the reverse has seven white stripes. As originally made, this militia color bore the British Union Jack in the canton like several other pre-1775 flags. It served Patriot troops on April 19, 1775, during the Alarm for Lexington and Concord, the first battles of the Revolution. Soon afterward, the British symbol was replaced by the stripes symbolizing America.

This unique standard predates the Declaration of Independence and the first national flag of the country. It probably survived in part because the coast off Manchester needed protection against the British and thus the town's militia company was not sent south after Massachusetts-Bay was liberated in 1776. The color was carefully preserved for 200 years by the descendants of Lieutenant Samuel Forster of the Essex Regiment, who had carried it in the Revolution. Today the flag is one of only approximately 30 known surviving American military colors from that war.

GALLERY I

Continental Colors

Date:
First quarter, 20th century (replica)

Size:
24.5" hoist x 36" fly

Medium:
Rayon; machine-stitched

Provenance:
Acquired by the Zaricor Flag Collection in 1996 from the Star-Spangled Banner Flag House Collection of Baltimore, MD.
ZFC0082

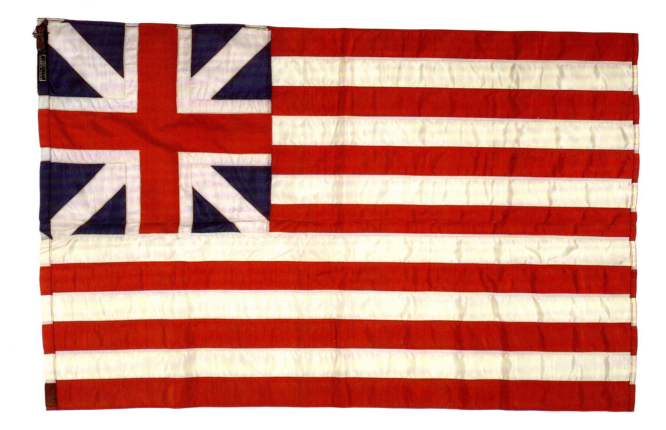

The Continental Colors was the first national flag of the United States, although never officially recognized by the 2nd Continental Congress. Its canton—the upper hoist quarter of the flag—bears a union of the crosses of St. George, symbolizing England, and St. Andrew, symbolizing Scotland. This indicated that Americans still professed loyalty to King George until independence was proclaimed in 1776. The field of alternating red and white horizontal stripes, a design possibly borrowed from the flag of the Sons of Liberty, expressed the unity of the 13 colonies seeking redress of their grievances against Parliament.

The Continental Colors is first known to have been raised during the siege of Boston in the winter of 1775–1776. However, because its canton bore the Union Jack, it was initially mistaken by the British as a symbol of submission! The Continental Colors served the United States as a naval ensign and as a garrison flag throughout 1776 and at least until September 1777, three months after the Stars & Stripes was adopted. It received the first salute to the American flag when the ship *Andrea Doria* was honored by Dutch authorities in the Caribbean in November 1776.

Declaration of Independence Commemorative Print

Date:
1824 – 1828 or earlier

Size:
29" wide x 32" long

Medium:
Printed cotton; hand-stitched

Provenance:
Acquired by the Zaricor Flag Collection in 1997 from the De Young Museum San Francisco CA Collection through Butterfield & Butterfield Auction House of San Francisco, CA.
ZFC0212

The Flag Resolution of June 14, 1777, that replaced the British Union Jack in the flag representing the United Colonies with a blue canton bearing the 13 stars of the independent United States, was the result of a political decision made nearly a year earlier. The Declaration of Independence was adopted by the Second Continental Congress on July 2, 1776, and first read to the public two days later on July 4th—now celebrated as America's Independence Day. Although it had long been read annually at commemorations on that day, a new appreciation for the document took hold just prior to its 50th anniversary in 1826. That was especially the case when the nation learned of the death of two of its principal authors—John Adams and Thomas Jefferson—on July 4th that year.

This commemorative weaving bears the text of the Declaration of Independence, the seals of the 13 original states, and vignettes of Presidents Washington, Adams, and Jefferson. There are also pictures of the Boston Tea Party, the surrender of General Gates at Saratoga, and an American eagle carrying a flag. Examples of the same print in blue and white survive and versions printed on paper are also known.

GALLERY I

13-Star, 12-Stripe United States Flag

Date:
About 1814 or earlier; modified in 1880

Size:
60" hoist x 103" fly

Media:
White cotton and red wool bunting stripes with various different pattern blue calico stars; hand-sewn with later machine-sewn additions

Provenance:
Acquired by the Zaricor Flag Collection in 2002 from the Mastai Flag Collection through auction at Sotheby's of New York City.
ZFC0624

Although this flag bears the inscription, "Hancock & English." on a white cotton panel machine-sewn to its fly end, technical analysis of the flag proper reveals that it was made a good deal earlier than the 1880 presidential campaign that brought those men —respectively the Democratic presidential and vice-presidential candidates—to the public's attention. Indeed, the technical and interpretative data of this flag suggest that it may be from earlier than the War of 1812.

This flag is clearly homemade and is characterized by several variations from the legal description of the U.S. flag. Its makers nevertheless captured the essence of the Stars & Stripes even though the amounts and colors of the cloth available to them caused them to reverse the standard canton and star colors, resulting in a white field with blue calico print stars. At some time in its use, the number of stripes was also reduced to twelve when the lowest—white—stripe was removed. It should be noted that such deficiencies in flag details were not uncommon in that era.

According to its previous owner, this flag was secured from a family in New England. However, it has many characteristics in common with the "Guilford flag" from North Carolina. Once thought to have been flown in the Revolution, that flag as a result of technical analysis now is generally dated to America's second war with England (1812–1814.)

Although not a common practice, reversal of the colors of the canton occasionally was employed. Notable examples include the U.S. Revenue Service ensign of 1799 and Captain John C. Frémont's flag of 1841. Such flags are now extremely rare.

GALLERY I

"Star of Bethlehem" Crib Quilt

Francis Hopkinson: Father of the U.S. Flag?

(Left)
Date:
About 1840 – 1900
Size:
59" wide x 59" long
Medium:
Cotton fabrics
Provenance:
Acquired by the Veninga Flag Collection in 1996.
LV02

(Right)
Oil painting, about 1765 – 1770
Courtesy of the National Portrait Gallery

1737 – 1791

While favoring a secular state that could help the country avoid the tragedies of religious persecution and warfare long characterizing Europe, most 19th century Americans in their personal lives exhibited strong religious beliefs. Not surprisingly, these were often reflected in homemade items such as wood carvings, samplers, paintings, and quilts. This example, manifesting the artistic imagination and technical skill that have since led to the recognition of quilts as a leading form of American folk art, shows the religious icon known as the "Star of Bethlehem."

As the Gospel of St. Matthew (2:1-2) relates, "There came wise men from the east to Jerusalem, saying…we have seen his star in the east, and are come to worship him." Scholars and divines have long argued over details of the story, but this quiltmaker had no doubts about its image. That star must be large, dazzling, unforgettable, and it must outshine all other stars in the heavens. Intentionally or not, the quilt also embodies the American national red, white, and blue colors.

The only person who registered a claim during the Revolution for having designed the original Stars & Stripes was Francis Hopkinson. His claim was turned down, not because his contemporaries didn't believe him, but because they thought that such "works of fancy" should be done by public servants as part of their regular responsibilities. Hopkinson was a judge and congressman, as well as a poet and heraldic artist. His designs were used for the seals of New Jersey and the Admiralty Board, although his conception for the Great Seal of the United States was not adopted.

Historians today, while lacking complete details of his work, are generally in agreement that Hopkinson was responsible for the original Stars & Stripes design. As a heraldist he may have chosen to arrange the stars in a ring, a recognized heraldic symbol he used in designing currency for the country. That would have been appropriate for "the new constellation" referred to in the Flag Act of 1777, suggesting the endless union of equal independent states.

13-Star United States Flag

Date:
1795 – 1820

Size:
50.5" hoist x 100" fly

Media:
Wool bunting with cotton stars; hand-sewn with later machine-stitched repairs

Provenance:
Acquired by the Zaricor Flag Collection in 2002 through auction at Sotheby's of New York City.

ZFC0604

The dating of this flag has been an enigma to those conservators and vexillologists who have studied it. Its 13 six-pointed stars are arranged in the form of a six-pointed "grand luminary." In both the overall configuration of the star pattern and in the utilization of six-pointed stars, that design duplicates the star arrangement in the 1782 Great Seal of the United States, as adopted by the Continental Congress.

The flag stars, however, are made of cotton, a material rarely if ever found in American flags until 1800. Moreover, the date of the thread used in hand-sewn sections of the flag, also of cotton, is open to contention. It was once thought to date no earlier than 1840, but more recently it has been hypothesized that cotton thread may have seen limited use 15 to 25 years earlier. While the two types of machine-stitching discovered in the stripes can date no earlier than 1850, these are repairs from a reuse of the flag in a later period. Accordingly, the "final chapter" on this flag has yet to be written.

Crest of the Great Seal of the United States

America's First Flag Makers
— Rebecca Young

(Left)
Date: 1781
Medium: Newsprint
Provenance: Newspaper advertisement for Rebecca Young which appeared in the Pennsylvania Packet of May 26, 1781. Courtesy of the Star-Spangled Banner Flag House Collection of Baltimore, MD.

(Right)
Date: 1876
Medium: Lithograph
Provenance: Acquired by the Zaricor Flag Collection in 1996 from the Star-Spangled Banner Flag House Collection of Baltimore, MD.
ZFC0640

ALL KINDS OF COLOURS, For the ARMY and NAVY, Made and Sold, on the most reasonable Terms, By Rebecca Young, In Walnut-street, near Third-street, and next door but one to Mr. Samuel M'Lane's. N. B. Any person having BUNTING for Sale, may hear of a Purchaser, by applying as above.

Elizabeth ("Betsy") Griscom, under her name from her first marriage—"Betsy Ross"—probably has the highest recognition factor of any woman in American history. She sewed flags during the Revolution for the Pennsylvania Navy, but these were not the 13-star Stars & Stripes. Well into the nineteenth century—under her name from her third marriage "Elizabeth Claypoole"—she continued to sew flags for the United States government. However, the claim made by her family a century later that she constructed the very first of the "Stars & Stripes" flags has not been substantiated and indeed most vexillologists (flag historians) question its accuracy.

Many other men and women also made flags during the Revolution and Federal Period. One of them, Rebecca Young, might be called "America's First flag maker." When her husband died during service with the Continental Army, she began work to support herself and her five children through her contacts with her brother, Colonel Benjamin Flower, a staff officer in charge of quartermaster supplies to the Continental Army. There are extensive records of the business she conducted from her homes in Philadelphia and—later—in Baltimore, making both silk and wool flags as well as other military supplies.

In 1807 Rebecca Young moved from Philadelphia to Baltimore, where she moved into the home of her daughter Mary Pickersgill.

Mary Pickersgill continued her mother's work and was responsible for making the original Star-Spangled Banner in the presence of her mother. Her niece Eliza, then 13, signed the receipt for that flag, which flew over Fort McHenry in 1814 and inspired Francis Scott Key to write the words to our national anthem. Mary's daughter Caroline and other family members were also involved in the business. Today the Star-Spangled Banner Flag House in Baltimore, where Pickersgill lived, is a museum that honors their work.

George Washington, Currier & Ives lithograph, "The Spirit of '76"

13-Star United States Flag, "Ring of Stars" Pattern

The "ring of stars"—or so-called "Betsy Ross pattern"—United States flag arranges 13 five-pointed stars in a circle, all pointing outward. This design was first popularized by Schuyler Hamilton in his 1853 *History of the National Flag of the United States of America*. In 1851 Emanuel Leutze, a German artist, had featured a Stars & Stripes of the same design in his painting *Washington Crossing the Delaware*, which later became well known to Americans. After 1870, when the grandson of Elizabeth "Betsy" Ross publicized his family's claim that she had created the five-pointed star and circular arrangement of stars, that pattern gained unjustified popular credence as the sole original Stars & Stripes of 1777–1795.

That belief was reinforced after the design appeared in two later paintings—Archibald M. Willard's *The Spirit of '76*, painted in 1876 in anticipation of the U.S. centennial, and C.H. Weisgerber's *Birth of Our Nation's Flag*, executed for the 1893 Columbian Exposition. Both depicted the Stars & Stripes in the "Betsy Ross design," with a circle of 13 five-pointed stars.

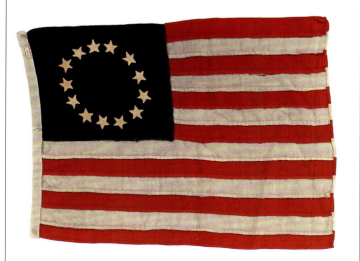

13-Star United States Merchant Ship Ensign

This flag is one of the earliest United States flags in the Zaricor Flag Collection. The use of cotton stars suggests production after 1799; the woolen stripes have selvedges typical of early power-loomed material and the flag is hand-stitched. It has been suggested that the flag could date even earlier than 1800. The marking "1½" on the flag's linen heading refers to a flag manufactured to a specific fly dimension—in this case one and a half yards or 54". As a result of extensive usage, the fly has been trimmed and resewn and is now only 48".

The size marking on the heading is more typical of flags manufactured as stock items rather than individually hand-crafted on special order. One of the earliest identified flag manufacturers in the United States was Rebecca Young of Philadelphia and Baltimore. She advertised in the newspapers around 1803 that she had on hand ready-made flags and this flag may be one of her products.

During the administration of President Thomas Jefferson (1801–1809) the United States purchased the Louisiana Territory from France. The Lewis and Clark Expedition during those years laid the basis for later American claims to sovereignty in the West.

(Left)
Date:
First quarter, 20th century (replica)
Size:
25.5" hoist x 32" fly
Medium:
Cotton; machine-stitched
Provenance:
Acquired by the Zaricor Flag Collection in 1996 from the Star-Spangled Banner Flag House Collection of Baltimore, MD.
ZFC0026

(Right)
Date:
Probably mid-Federal Period (1800 – 1805)
Size:
31" hoist x 48.5" fly
Media:
Wool bunting and cotton stars; hand-stitched
Provenance:
Acquired by the Zaricor Flag Collection in 1992 from William Guthman of Westport, CT.
ZFC0419

GALLERY I

13-Star United States Flag

Date:
About 1845 – 1850

Size:
69" hoist x 105" fly

Medium:
Cotton; hand-sewn

Provenance:
Acquired by the Zaricor Flag Collection in 1996 from Wesley Cowan Auction of Cincinnati, OH.
ZFC1495

This flag is made completely of cotton—with its stars arranged in a circle around a larger center star. The canton is relatively small and rests on a red stripe. Moreover, this flag was once secured to a halyard used to hoist it by means of ties sewn to or attached through the rings along the cotton heading. Because of its many similar production techniques, it has been suggested that it was made by a Philadelphia maker. It is likely that this flag dates from no earlier than 1840, but it may be earlier. At least two militia flags made during the War with Mexico also display their stars in a circle around a central star and this flag may date from the same period.

James K. Polk was U.S. president under more versions of the Stars & Stripes than any other president. There were 26 stars when he was inaugurated in March 1845 and new flags with additional stars to honor new states were created that year (for Florida's admission) as well as in 1846, 1847, and 1848 (for the admission of Texas, Iowa, and Wisconsin.)

13-Star United States Flag

Date:
About 1850 – 1870

Size:
57" hoist x 115" fly

Medium:
Cotton; machine-sewn with hand-sewn stars

Provenance:
Acquired by the Zaricor Flag Collection in 1996 from the Wesley Cowan Auction of Cincinnati, OH.
ZFC0359

This flag is very similar in both design and size to the No. 10 size U.S. Navy boat flag. However, because it is made from cotton and is machine-sewn, it clearly is not a Navy flag from the period when the 4-5-4 pattern boat flags were in service (1862–1870).

While this flag may have been made for the Centennial celebrations of 1876, a star pattern more in vogue at that time consisted of five staggered rows of 3-2-3-2-3 stars. The use of cotton and the absence of brass grommets suggest that the flag was privately, rather than commercially made. It is possible that this was produced for some patriotic purpose during the Civil War.

13-Star United States Flag

Date:
About 1876

Size:
43" hoist x 96" fly

Media:
Wool bunting with cotton stars; machine-stitched with hand-stitched stars

Provenance:
Acquired by the Zaricor Flag Collection in 1998 from Butterfield & Butterfield Auction House of San Francisco, CA. ZFC1156

The 13-star United States flag with its stars arranged in five staggered horizontal rows, 3-2-3-2-3, is one of the two basic star patterns known to have been utilized by the U.S. Navy during the Revolutionary War. A 1779 painting made in the Dutch harbor of Texel depicts the ensign of the *Alliance* with the stars arranged in this pattern.

Beginning at some time during the American Civil War, this pattern was resurrected for the star field on some of the U.S. Navy boat flags. After the War, it became the predominant pattern—until 1870—and then the sole star pattern until boat flags were discontinued in 1916. This flag, however, does not conform to any of the sizes specified for Navy boat flags and is probably a flag of commercial manufacture, probably constructed at the time of the United States Centennial celebrations in Philadelphia, Pennsylvania, which were attended by President Ulysses S. Grant.

13-Star United States Navy Boat Flag, Size No. 12

Date:
About 1863 – 1865

Size:
46.5" hoist x 84" fly

Media:
Wool bunting with cotton stars; hand-sewn, canvas heading with brass grommets

Provenance:
Acquired by the Zaricor Flag Collection in 2002 from the Mastai Flag Collection through auction at Sotheby's of New York City.

ZFC0632

13-Star United States Flag

With allowance for loose tolerances and shrinkage, this 13-star United States flag conforms to the dimensions specified from 1863 through 1882 for the No. 12 size, 7-foot fly dimension, boat flag. The panel later attached to the flag indicates that it saw Civil War service, although on what ship has not been recorded.

The heading bears a pair of brass grommets. Although such grommets began to be popular substitutes to supplant hand-sewn buttonhole eyelets among commercial flag manufacturers in the 1860s, they were not employed on U.S. Navy boat flags until the 1890s. Hence, it is believed that this flag was furnished to the U.S. Navy during the American Civil War by a contract flag-maker.

Abraham Lincoln became president in 1861. Following his assassination four years later, just as the Civil War was ending in the Spring of 1865, Vice President Andrew Johnson succeeded him. The 13th amendment to the Constitution, which ended slavery, was ratified in December that year.

The 13-star United States flag with its stars arranged in the 3-2-3-2-3 pattern was the version most often illustrated in the flag identification charts published in Europe after the 1783 Treaty of Paris, which recognized American independence. That pattern seems to have been revived during the American Civil War. Because it symmetrically filled the canton, the pattern also became an increasingly popular commemorative flag during the decade leading up to the Centennial celebration. This flag would have been flown during the administration of Ulysses S. Grant.

A small, oar powered, launch is shown bearing a U.S. navy boat flag at its stern in this 1864 photograph of the U.S.S. Commodore Morris.

(Left)
Date:
1864
Medium:
Black and white photograph
Provenance:
From the U.S. Army Military History Institute Archives

(Right)
Date:
About 1876
Size:
36" hoist x 57" fly
Media:
Wool bunting with cotton stars; machine-sewn with machine-stitched stars
Provenance:
Acquired by the Zaricor Flag Collection in 1999 from Scott Guthman of Santa Cruz, CA, who acquired it from his father William Guthman of Connecticut
ZFC1091

What Is a "Navy Boat Flag"?

Date:
1865

Medium:
Black and white drawing

Provenance:
Sketch by Charles E. Stedman showing boat flags displayed from the launches sent to resupply the blockading vessels of the U.S. Navy. Courtesy of the U.S. Army Military History Institute Photo Archives.

The flag that identifies the nationality of a major fighting ship is known as its "ensign" and is flown from a staff or halyard at the stern of a vessel. For ships of the United States Navy, the ensign is the Stars & Stripes. Depending on the rating (which varied with the size, number of cannon, and masts) a U.S. Navy vessel might have several sizes of ensigns to fly during ordinary or special occasions.

During the period of the sailing navy and the early steam-powered navy, nearly all ships possessed small boats, known as gigs, propelled by oars or small sails. These gigs permitted the transfer of personnel or small cargos from ship to shore or ship to ship on the open sea. Like their mother ships, these gigs or small boats carried a stern staff for a small ensign. The small ensigns flown on these gigs were called boat flags by the U.S. Navy and usually were made in five sizes. The common fly widths for these small flags varied from five feet through ten feet.

When first employed, boat flags followed the same pattern and design as the current ensigns of the ship. However, as the number of states increased, so too did the number of stars on both the ensigns and the boat flags. For the large ensigns, this posed little problem; the flags were large enough that the stars were still visible. For the small boat flags, however, the corresponding diminishing of the star size as the number of stars grew meant that the stars in the union tended to blur, affecting the recognition of the flag.

Until at least 1854, U.S. Navy boat flags still continued to bear the full complement of 31 stars. However, by 1857, a decision had been made to reduce the star count in boat flags so as to retain the stars' visibility. At first the number was reduced to 16, a number chosen most likely for practicality rather than any specific significance. In late 1861 or early 1862, however, the Navy Department further reduced the number of stars to 13, in effect recreating the old naval flag of the American War for Independence. These were initially arranged in three horizontal rows, the rows bearing four, five, and four stars respectively. During the Civil War, it is thought that Navy contractors introduced a different star pattern that also harked back to the Revolution. These boat flags had a star arrangement consisting of five horizontal rows, the number of stars being staggered—three, two, three, two, and three. By 1870, this pattern had emerged as the predominant arrangement for boat flags.

In 1882, the number of boat flag sizes was reduced from five to three, although near the turn of the 20th century, a fourth, even smaller, size was added. The 13-star boat flag continued in use until 1916, when the Secretary of the Navy reinstated the United States flag with a full complement of stars for all ensigns aboard U.S. Navy ships.

A NEW CONSTELLATION

13-Star United States Navy Boat Flag, Size No. 12

Date:
About 1862–1863

Size:
47" hoist x 84" fly

Media:
Wool bunting with cotton stars; hand-sewn

Provenance:
Acquired by the Zaricor Flag Collection in 2002 from the Mastai Flag Collection through auction at Sotheby's of New York City.

ZFC0614

This U.S. Navy ensign carries 13 stars in the 4-5-4 arrangement that has been documented as one of the two most common star patterns flown aboard U.S. Navy ships during the Revolutionary War. However, the star pattern also conforms to the design of flags flown aboard U.S. Navy small boats during the period of the American Civil War and immediately thereafter. Indeed the measurement along the fly of the flag (84") conforms exactly to the size prescribed for the size No. 12 ensign in the 1863–1864 regulations. The U.S. Navy produced boat flags with 13 stars arranged in the 4-5-4 pattern from 1862 until about 1870, after which another popular pattern predominated.

Why Is This Flag "Reversed"?
The 1942 Flag Code specifies that the United States flag, when displayed on a wall, show the side which the viewer sees when the canton (union with the stars) is to his or her left. The Flag Code is intended for the proper display of contemporary flags, and was not written to forbid the display of historic flags whose reverse sides may bear significant details otherwise obscured if shown in accordance with the code, such is the case with this flag.

13-Star United States Navy Boat Flag, Size No. 14

Date:
1866–1870

Size:
30" hoist x 57" fly

Medium:
Wool bunting with red and blue elements press-dyed; hand-sewn sections

Provenance:
Acquired by the Zaricor Flag Collection in 1996 from the Star-Spangled Banner Flag House Collection of Baltimore, MD.
ZFC0013

No wool bunting, the preferred fabric for making flags, was manufactured in the United States until 1865. Until then all bunting was imported from England, where the cottage industry—later replaced by machine looms—in the Sudbury area had specialized in making that fabric. During the American Civil War, the demand for United States flags reached unprecedented heights, but U.S. relations with England remained strained during the conflict.

In early 1865 Benjamin Butler, after a checkered Army career, promoted legislation requiring all flags for the military to be constructed with American-made bunting. The legislation was self-serving, as he had begun to form the United States Bunting Company in Lowell, Massachusetts, together with D.W.C. Farrington. In addition to co-founding that firm, Farrington controlled Holt's patents for resist (or press) dyeing of fabrics. In 1865–1866 the U.S. Bunting Company proposed to make all the flags needed by the Army and the Navy. The Army had a substantial supply in stock at the War's end, but the Navy accepted the company's offer. This size No.14 boat flag still bears the marks of the United States Bunting Company on its heading.

Detail of heading with "U.S. Bunting Co." stamp

13-Star United States Navy Boat Flag, Size No. 14

Date:
1868 – 1870

Size:
30" hoist x 57" fly

Medium:
Wool bunting with red and blue elements press-dyed; hand-sewn sections

Provenance:
Acquired by the Zaricor Flag Collection in 2002 from the Mastai Flag Collection through auction at Sotheby's of New York City.
ZFC0633

During the American Civil War as the United States Navy mushroomed in size, the demand for flags exceeded the Navy's ability to furnish flags through the various U.S. Navy Yards located at key ports along the Atlantic. Historians have speculated that the Navy Yards turned to civilian contractors to make up the deficit. While the Navy Yard boat flags were sewn with the stars arranged in three horizontal rows of 4-5-4, it appears that those supplied by the contractors followed a different Navy tradition, arranging them in five staggered horizontal rows of 3-2-3-2-3.

Sewing the stars to each side of the canton was tedious work. After the Civil War one of the contracting firms produced the star pattern with a "press block" or "resist-dyeing" technique that had been patented with improvements made by John Holt. The separate canton section of the field was placed in a block that prevented the areas that were to show as white stars from receiving the blue indigo dye. The same technique of blocking out areas of the striped field, so that only alternate strips of red would accept the dye, created two sections for the 13 stripes. All three elements would then be sewn together by hand to make an inexpensive flag.

GALLERY I

13-Star United States
Navy Boat Flag, Size No. 7

Date:
1891

Size:
35" hoist x 64" fly

Media:
Wool bunting with cotton stars; hand-sewn

Provenance:
Acquired by the Zaricor Flag Collection in 2002 from the Mastai Flag Collection through auction at Sotheby's of New York City.

ZFC0683

Detail of heading

During the last three decades of the 19th century and through 1916, the "boat flags" made by or for the United States Navy bore 13 stars arranged in a staggered pattern of five horizontal rows of 3-2-3-2-3. The 1882 Navy regulations provided for three sizes of boat flags, the No. 6, the No. 7, and the No. 8, which respectively measured on the fly 80", 66", and 54". The heading of this flag is stenciled with the size marking "U.S. Ensign No. 7."

In addition the heading indicates that the flag was made at the Navy Yard N.Y. in Brooklyn in April 1891. For the last 25 years of their production, the headings of U.S. Navy boat flags would incorporate these manufacturing data—to the great aid of future flag historians.

The period immediately preceding and following the year this flag was manufactured for the Navy were politically volatile.

Benjamin Harrison defeated Democratic incumbent Grover Cleveland in the 1888 presidential election. Harrison won the electoral college majority although, like Lincoln in 1860 and Hayes in 1876, he failed to obtain a majority of the popular vote. Cleveland ran against Harrison again in 1892, winning the only non-consecutive second term in U.S. history.

During these decades the U.S. Navy took its hesitant steps to the development of the steel-hulled ships that would form the basis of "The Great White Fleet."

A New Star for Every State

The Flag Act of 1794

"Be it enacted, etc., that from and after the first day of May, one thousand seven hundred and ninety-five, the flag of the United States be fifteen stripes alternate red and white; that the union be fifteen stars, white in a blue field."
—Flag Act of March 27, 1794

In October 1780, to foster the transfer of "western" territorial claims held by seven of the original thirteen colonies, Continental Congress adopted a resolution promising that the national government would administer these western lands for the common good, and "that new states would be carved from these territories who would have equal footing with the original thirteen."

The groundwork laid in 1780 came to fruition a decade later under the newly adopted Constitution when Vermont, previously claimed by both New Hampshire and New York, and Kentucky, formerly claimed by Virginia, became the 14th and 15th states, respectively on March 4, 1791 and June 1, 1792.

On the day after Christmas, 1793, Vermont Senator Stephen R. Bradley introduced a resolution to change the United States flag to a field of 15 stripes with a blue union bearing an equal number of stars. While the resolution passed the Senate without debate, when it came to the floor of the House of Representatives, the resolution stirred up a plethora of negative commentary. Some congressmen belittled the proposal as entirely unworthy as their first consideration of the new session. Others, especially those invested in seafaring trade, complained that the change would cost each ship owner no less than $60.00 per ship for re-equipping vessels. After discussing the bill further, on the 13th of January 1794 the House adopted the new flag act by a margin of eight votes. Despite further admissions of states, this act would define the "official" national flag for the next 23 years.

That legislation was the first to officially recognize more than 13 stripes for the flag. Both the Treasury Department and the Indian Department later officially used flags of more than 15 stripes.

United States
Revenue Cutter Service Ensign & Pennant

On March 2, 1799, Congress authorized "cutters and boats employed in the service of the revenue" for the United States Treasury Department to fly a distinctive ensign and masthead pennant. On August 1st of that year, the Secretary of the Treasury defined those flags: "The ensign and pendant…consists of sixteen perpendicular stripes alternate red and white, the union of the ensign bearing the arms of the United States in dark blue on a white field." Until 1915, flags of this style identified those U.S. ships engaged on customs and revenue service; after 1915 the same flag—with the addition of the Coast Guard insignia on the stripes—was flown by the Revenue Cutter Service's successor, the United States Coast Guard.

The Customs Service continues to use a modernized version of this flag.

When the Revenue Cutter Service flags were adopted, 16 states comprised the Union. Although Ohio became the 17th state in 1803, no change was made in the Revenue Service flags. Nevertheless, the utilization of 16 stripes reflects the pervading concept that the number of stripes be increased with every addition of a new state. The Indian Department, then a branch of the War Department, also adopted a distinctive flag with the coat of arms of the U.S. in its canton.

(Top)
Date:
About 1870 – 1880
Size:
80" hoist x 144" fly
Media:
Wool bunting stripes and canton, cotton stars and coat of arms; hand sewn
Provenance:
Flag acquired by the Zaricor Flag Collection in 2002 from the Mastai Flag Collection through auction at Sotheby's of New York City.
ZFC0620

(Bottom)
Date:
About 1890s
Size:
2" hoist x 60" fly
Medium:
Wool bunting; press dyed
Provenance:
Flag acquired by the Zaricor Flag Collection in 2002 from the Mastai Flag Collection through auction at Sotheby's of New York City.
ZFC0637

15-Star United States Flag

Date:
1803 – 1812 / 1812 – 1816

Size:
108" hoist x 112" fly

Media:
Wool bunting and linen stars, all hand-sewn

Provenance:
Acquired by the Zaricor Flag Collection in 1997 from Norm Flayderman of Ft. Lauderdale, FL, previously from whaling collection of W.H. Bartlett, New Bedford, MA.
ZFC0418

Flag traditions of the United States Navy and of the U.S. merchant fleet are largely based on the practices of the Royal Navy and merchant marine of Great Britain. In the late 18th century the British Union Jack—a combination of the crosses of St. George and St. Andrew—flew on the jackstaff at the prow of British ships, while its design appeared in the canton of various ensigns hoisted at the stern of those vessels. The U.S. ensign bore a field of stripes with a canton of blue bearing white stars. The design and size of the jack corresponded to the canton of that ensign.

This flag now bears 15 stars in three horizontal rows of 5 stars each, corresponding to the "official" U.S. jack for 1795–1818. At some point it may have borne two or three more stars. Only the tip of one of those stars still remains, hidden in the (shortened) fly hem. The linen heading of this flag bears the inscription "Ship Vinyard." This may be a reference to a sailing schooner of that name that plied between New York and Baltimore in the employ of the Regular Line, a shipping company in business in the first half of the 19th century.

Unofficial Flags of the U.S. 1795–1818

"Mr. Wendover then stated the incongruity of the flags in general use (except those in the Navy), not agreeing with the law and generally varying from each other. He instanced the flags then flying over the building in which Congress sat, and that at the Navy Yard, one of which contained only nine stripes, the other eighteen, and neither conforming to the law."
—British Naval Chronicle, 1817

As the debate over the proposed changes to the United States flag came to an end in 1794, one of the representatives in the House offered an amendment that would make this change "permanent." Although this amendment failed, the flag that became the official symbol of the nation on May 1, 1795, did not change legally for the next 23 years. Proportions and star arrangements might vary, but surviving examples from ships of the U.S. Navy and from coastal and inland fortifications displayed 15 stripes and a union bearing 15 stars. The most famous of these flags flew over Fort McHenry in Baltimore Harbor during the British bombardment in September of 1814, the sight of which prompted Francis Scott Key to pen the poem "The Star-Spangled Banner" (afterwards put to music and in 1931 officially denominated the national anthem).

While the 15-stripe, 15-star flag was the official symbol identifying the properties of the Navy and War Departments of the U.S. government, at least two other government agencies—the Treasury Department and the Indian Department—adopted flags that conformed to the spirit of the 1794 flag act if not the letter.

As four other states were admitted to the Union—Tennessee as the 16th on June 1, 1796; Ohio as the 17th on March 1, 1803; Louisiana as the 18th on April 30, 1812, and Indiana as the 19th on December 11, 1816—the general populace and the makers commissioned to produce flags followed the spirit of the 1794 enactment by producing flags that added either stars only or both stars and stripes that reflected the current number of states in the Union.

Flags survive—or have been documented to have existed—bearing sixteen stars and sixteen stripes, seventeen stars and seventeen stripes, and eighteen stars and eighteen stripes! At the same time other flag makers—in order to retain the aesthetics of the Stars & Stripes—merely added stars to the old design, so that thirteen—and fifteen—stripe flags survive with sixteen, seventeen, and eighteen stars. Flag making had become an art.

1802 oil painting depicting the launching of the sailing ship Fame *at Salem, Massachusetts; courtesy of the Peabody Essex Museum, Salem, MA*

16-Star, 13-Stripe "Grand Luminary" United States Flag

Date:
Mid-Federal Period (1796 – 1803)

Size:
55" hoist x 85.5" fly

16 Stars:
Unofficial (Tennessee statehood June 1, 1796)

Media:
Wool bunting with cotton stars; hand-sewn with linen thread

Provenance:
Acquired by the Zaricor Flag Collection in 1997, formerly in the Norm Flayderman Collection.
ZFC0420

Although no flag with 16, 17, 18, or 19 stars was ever formally adopted by Congress, the spirit of the 1794 flag resolution led numerous patrons in need of a United States flag to order one that included newly recognized states. Such flags added an extra star—and sometimes a stripe—to the then current U.S. flag. This flag conforms to that spirit.

The linen thread with which the flag is sewn indicates a product predating the widespread distribution of cotton thread, although the stars are cut from cotton fabric which was not reasonably priced until after 1800. The 16 stars are arranged in the form of a "grand luminary"—a design championed by Captain Samuel C. Reid in 1817. He held it to be the star pattern that would best represent the concept *E Pluribus Unum*, the national motto—"Out of Many, One." This is possibly an early merchant ship ensign from the period 1796 – 1803.

This flag served during the presidencies of either George Washington, John Adams and/or Thomas Jefferson.

16-Star United States Flag

Dates:
(1802) 1812 – 1818 (1840)
Size:
52.5" hoist x 117" fly
16 Stars:
Unofficial (Tennessee statehood June 1, 1796)
Medium:
Cotton; hand-stitched
Provenance:
Acquired by the Zaricor Flag Collection in 1996 from the Star-Spangled Banner Flag House Collection of Baltimore, MD., who obtained it in 1964 from Academy of Natural Sciences of Philadelphia.
ZFC0423

According to the documentation of this flag's provenance, it was the first flag flown over the Academy of Natural Sciences of Philadelphia. That institution was founded in 1812, when the nation was comprised of 17, and then 18 states. However, this flag bears only 16 stars, more appropriate to the period 1796–1802, consequent to Tennessee's admission to the Union.

The flag also has an association with the Vaux family of Philadelphia. William S. Vaux (1811–1882) was a noted mineralogist who made donations to the Academy. His son George was Treasurer of the Academy at the turn of the 20th century. It has been suggested that this may have been a Vaux family flag, predating the formation of the Academy. However, the earliest date for the manufacture of the sewing thread used in the construction of this flag is in dispute. Until further research is conducted on the dating of cotton sewing threads, any verdict regarding the date of this flag is speculative.

In 1812, when the Academy was founded, the U.S. president was James Madison.

17-Star, 13-Stripe United States Flag

(Left)
Date:
Mid-Federal Period (1803 – 1812)
Size:
32" hoist x 47" fly
17 Stars:
Unofficial (Ohio statehood March 1, 1803)
Media:
Wool bunting with cotton stars; hand-sewn
Provenance:
Acquired by the Zaricor Flag Collection in 2002 from the Mastai Flag Collection through auction at Sotheby's of New York City.
ZFC0626

Ohio achieved its statehood in 1803 as the 17th state in the Union, yet no alteration was made in the nation's flag at that time. The 15-star, 15-stripe version adopted in 1794 remained the official flag of the nation until 1818. It is known, however, that the United States Indian Department ordered 17-star, 17-stripe flags in the period 1804–1805 and later. Privately-made flags from the same era also tended to reflect a consensus that all the states should be represented in the U.S. flag.

This flag, bearing 16 small stars in an oval around a central star—presumably representing Ohio—would seem to conform to that concept. Also, there are known surviving 13-star flags, also dating to the mid-Federal Period, likewise characterized by this same basic star pattern. Neither the presidency of Thomas Jefferson nor James Madison supported any effort to standardize the flag. A regulation star arrangement still lay a century in the future.

20-Star United States Navy Boat Flag

(Right)
Date:
1818
Size:
39.5" hoist x 72" fly
20 Stars:
July 4, 1818 – July 3, 1819 (statehood: Tennessee June 1, 1796; Ohio March 1, 1803; Louisiana April 30, 1812; Indiana December 11, 1816; Mississippi December 10, 1817)
Media:
Wool bunting with cotton stars
Provenance:
Acquired by the Zaricor Flag Collection in 1997, formerly in the Flayderman Collection.
ZFC0421

With the close of the Revolutionary War, the Continental Congress dismantled the naval forces that it and the states had raised. However, in 1798 a war with France seemed imminent and consequently the new Congress re-authorized the United States Navy. During the War of 1812 with Great Britain, the Navy performed gallantly and Congress did not disband it after the conflict ended.

In the early 19th century the Navy Department assigned squadrons of warships to patrol areas of the Atlantic Ocean to protect American commercial interests. The ships of these squadrons usually returned to a specific homeport where navy yards had been established for the construction and refitting of vessels.

The smallest flags made at these navy yards were for the small oar-powered boats carried on larger vessels. This "6-foot ensign" was six feet long. As one of the smallest of the flags made by the Navy, it qualified as a boat flag. The stars are arranged in four aligned horizontal rows of five stars each, as specified in the Navy circular issued on September 10, 1818, during the presidency of James Monroe.

A Delicate Balance

"Be it enacted & c., that from and after the fourth day of July next, the flag of the United States be thirteen horizontal stripes, alternate red and white; that the union have twenty stars, white, in a blue field."
— *First section of the Flag Act of April 4, 1818*

In the two decades following the adoption of the flag act of 1794, three new states—Tennessee on June 1, 1796; Ohio on March 1, 1803, and Louisiana on April 30, 1812—were admitted to the United States. Following the conclusion of the second War with Great Britain (1812 – 1815), Indiana was admitted on December 11, 1816, and Mississippi Territory seemingly lay ahead on the brink of admission. Still, the official flag of the United States consisted of only 15 stripes and only 15 stars.

The lack of recognition for new states prompted New York Congressman Peter Wendover to suggest that a committee be established to redesign the flag so as to accommodate the new states. The committee was created, but the brevity of the 1817 session delayed action on its proposal until the new session of 1818. In the interim, Mississippi had been admitted to the Union as the 20th state on December 10, 1817. After debate on the 24th and 25th of March, 1818, the act changing the Stars & Stripes to a flag of 13 horizontal stripes and a union bearing 20 stars was adopted.

The Flag Act of 1818 established a new principle that took further discussions out of Congressional hands. The second section of the act provided for any future additions of new states: "that on the admission of every new state into the union, one star be added to the union of the flag; and that such addition shall take effect on the fourth of July next succeeding such admission." The reduction of the number of stripes to 13 and the automatic admission of a new star was a concession to those who wished a permanent return to the flag of 13-stripes and 13-stars and at the same time a compromise with those who foresaw that the continued increase in the number of stripes would soon effectively change the character of the United States flag.

The compromise that resulted in the third—and final—enactment defining the United States flag was overshadowed by a more significant compromise. Throughout the last quarter of the 18th and the first quarter of the 19th centuries, the controversy over slavery simmered under the surface of the national agenda. During the 40 years between the Declaration of Independence the adoption of the third flag act, a balance had been maintained between states that recognized the institution of slavery and those that forbade it. Mississippi's admission balanced Indiana's at ten states each. Illinois—the next state admitted on December 3, 1818—was balanced by Alabama's admission as a slave state on December 14, 1819. The extension of slavery beyond the Mississippi River was addressed by Congress in 1820, and was part of what became known as the Missouri Compromise.

20-Star United States Flag, 1818

Acquired by the Zaricor Flag Collection in 2002 from the Mastai Flag Collection through auction at Sotheby's of New York City.
ZFC0625

21-Star "Grand Luminary" United States Flag

Date:
1819 – 1820

Size:
76.5" hoist x 89" fly

21 Stars:
*July 4, 1819 – July 3, 1820
(Illinois statehood
December 3, 1818)*

Media:
Cotton; hand-sewn

Provenance:
Acquired by the Zaricor Flag Collection in 1997, formerly in the Norm Flayderman Collection.
ZFC0422

Following Illinois' admission into the Union, in accordance with the provisions of the Flag Act of 1818 a new United States flag with 21 stars became official. The makers of this specific flag evidently were unable to secure bunting for constructing it and made it entirely of cotton. Rather than beginning with a red stripe, they chose to commence the alternating stripes with a white one. Although commencing and ending the American flag with horizontal red stripes was fast becoming the established practice, nothing in the relevant legislation specified that the red stripes were to take precedence.

The flag's makers chose to arrange the stars in the shape of a "Grand Luminary." The star design had been popularized by Captain Samuel C. Reid during the debate over the 1818 Flag Act. His wife had sewn the first flag that flew over Congress. While Mrs. Reid's flag bore the Grand Luminary arrangement, Congress chose not to incorporate that star pattern into its legislation. Nevertheless, that distinctive design remained popular among flag manufacturers for another 60 years. This flag was fabricated during the presidency of James Monroe.

E Pluribus Unum (Out of Many, One)

Samuel C. Reid 1783–1861

"The majority of the ships [in New York Harbor] had the stars arranged in five horizontal rows of six stars each, making thirty stars in all—thirty one being the proper number at the date. Some had one large star formed of thirty-one small stars, and this style prevailed in places of public amusement, and over the hotels of New York and Jersey City. Other vessels had them in lozenge, a diamond, or a circle."
— *Comments of Mr. S. Alofsen,*
Historical Magazine, *1857*

Although Congressman Peter Wendover was responsible for promoting the concept of a "new" Stars & Stripes, he did not actually design the flag. For that, Wendover had turned to Captain Samuel C. Reid, who had commanded the privateer *General Armstrong* during the recent War with England (1812–1814). The design that Reid submitted consisted of 13 alternating red and white horizontal stripes and a blue union bearing 20 white stars. Moreover, Reid's design also called for a special arrangement of the stars. For government vessels, the 20 stars were to be set in rows, as had been the tradition since the War for Independence. For private merchant ships and government buildings or installations, however, Reid had proposed that the 20 stars be arranged into a large single star configuration. This "Grand Luminary" as he called it, would symbolize the national motto, *E Pluribus Unum*—"Out of Many, One." Indeed, to demonstrate this design, Wendover had Mrs. Reid make such a flag to be shown to Congress. When the enactment was finally adopted, that flag was the first in accordance with the new legislation to fly over Congress on April 13, 1818.

While the "grand luminary" graced the first of the new flags to fly over Congress, no part of the actual legislation specified that arrangement. As in prior years, the arrangement of the stars was left to the imagination of the makers of the flags. While the "grand luminary" had no official standing, for the next six decades in American flag making, it would be one of several popular designs for the arrangement of the stars. It proved especially so when the number of the stars was an odd number or a number that refused to comfortably fit into even or staggered rows.

Date:
1880
Medium:
Woodcut
Provenance:
Engraving of Samuel C. Reid from Admiral George Henry Preble's History of the Flag of the United States of America, *1880.*

GALLERY II

26-Star "Grand Luminary—Shooting Star" United States Flag

Date:
About 1837 – 1845

Size:
113" hoist x 210" fly

26 Stars:
July 4, 1837 – July 3, 1844 (Michigan statehood January 26, 1837)

Media:
Wool bunting with cotton stars, hand-sewn

Provenance:
Acquired by the Zaricor Flag Collection in 2002 from the Mastai Flag Collection through auction at Sotheby's of New York City.
ZFC0606

Overwhelmingly, old flags come without any documentation about their date of construction, ownership over the years, and the design symbolism intended by the maker. Nevertheless careful analysis of large numbers of flags by conservators and vexillologists (flag historians) makes it possible to establish certain principles that can be applied in analyzing newly-found flags. Fortunately, variations in design characteristics are much more likely to be found in old American flags than in those from other countries.

This 26-star Stars & Stripes has the name "S. Gildersleeve" written on its heading. In 1828 Sylvester Gildersleeve created the Gildersleeve Shipbuilding Company in Portland, Connecticut, although his family had been doing work in that profession since the 18th century. This flag was probably associated with one of their vessels, although it is too early to have been made for the ship *S. Gildersleeve* which was constructed in 1854 and burned by the *C.S.S. Alabama* during the Civil War.

Collector Boleslaw Mastai attributed fanciful names to star patterns appearing on his flags. Most of these names are not known to have been used historically. He called this the "Gildersleeve Comet Flag" and saw it "rushing headlong into space, trailing its stars of glory." While the star pattern does not seem arbitrary, other interpretations of its symbolism are possible.

This flag was in use during the presidencies of either Martin Van Buren, William Henry Harrison and/or John Tyler.

26-Star United States Flag

Date:
1837 – 1845

Size:
23.5" hoist x 35" fly

26 Stars:
July 4, 1837 – July 3, 1845 (Michigan statehood January 26, 1837)

Medium:
Printed silk

Provenance:
Acquired by the Zaricor Flag Collection in 2002 from the Mastai Flag Collection through auction at Sotheby's of New York City.
ZFC0634

Printing color on silk or cotton fabrics initially employed wooden blocks that were hand-cut in order to leave a raised surface bearing the desired pattern. That design would be covered with ink or dye and pressed down on a piece of fabric, leaving an impression made by the raised section of the block. Finding wood whose surface was sufficiently porous to hold the right amount of dye proved difficult. Too little or too much dye could result in a ruined impression. An alternate technique used the raised area to press down on the fabric to prevent the dye from penetrating into the pressed-upon surface; this process was known as press-dyeing.

Another technique covered the raised surface with wax or some similar substance that was applied to the fabric, causing it to resist the dyes added afterward; this was known as "resist-dyeing." Neither system worked very well with fabrics until improvements were effected and patented by John Holt in the period 1865–1870. Nevertheless presentable, inexpensive flags were made by these processes in the two decades before Holt's improvements became available.

27-Star United States Flag

Date:
1845 – 1846

Size:
74" hoist x 134" fly

27 Stars:
*July 4, 1845 – July 3, 1846
(Florida statehood
March 3, 1845)*

Media:
*Wool bunting with cotton stars;
hand-sewn*

Provenance:
*Acquired by the Zaricor Flag
Collection in 1995 from
Hank Ford of Bedford,
New Hampshire.
ZFC1452*

The Territory of Florida, which the United States had purchased from Spain in 1819, achieved statehood on March 3, 1845. The star representing the new state was officially added to the union of the United States flag on July 4th of that year. However, since Texas was admitted as the 28th state later that same year, the 27-star flag became obsolete on Independence Day in 1846.

This particular flag bears the inked name "C.H. Green" inscribed on its white canvas heading. He is likely to have been the original owner of the flag or an individual who later acquired it. At nearly six feet by eleven feet, it is likely that this was utilized as a merchant ship ensign.

In 1846 the United States, under the leadership of James K. Polk, went to war with Mexico, and the American settlers in California proclaimed the "Bear Flag Republic" shortly before the area was seized by United States naval officers. The American star was used as a symbol on both the Texas and California flags.

GALLERY II

28-Star "Grand Luminary" United States National Color

Date:
1846

Size:
46.5" hoist x 80" fly

28 Stars:
July 4, 1846 – July 3, 1847 (Texas statehood December 29, 1845)

Medium:
Silk with painted stars; hand-sewn

Provenance:
Acquired by the Zaricor Flag Collection in 1996 from the Star-Spangled Banner Flag House Collection of Baltimore, MD.
ZFC1444

A NEW STAR

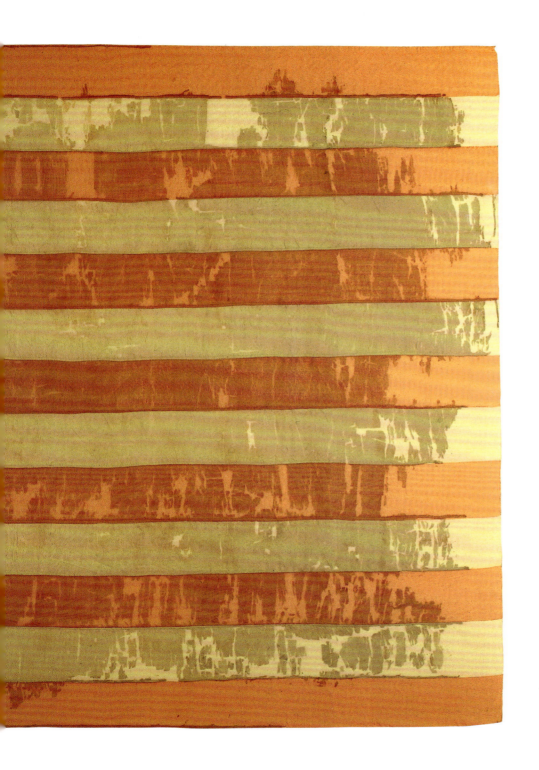

This United States national color was prepared by "the ladies of New Orleans" in May of 1846 for the 4th Regiment Louisiana Militia. The regiment, known as the "Montezuma Regiment," was organized for service in Mexico during 1846, but it was disbanded after only six months before seeing any combat. As often happened in that era, the unit commander, Colonel Horatio Davis, simply took the flag home with him when his unit was mustered out of service. Colonel (later General) Horatio Davis was born on the ship *Guerrière*, and his father, Samuel B. Davis, had been a "War of 1812 Old Defender" who had participated in the defense of Baltimore in 1814.

The 28 stars of this flag are painted in gold, as was common then. They form a single large star or "Grand Luminary" in the canton of the flag. The women who prepared it ignored—or more likely were unaware of—the official regulations for the preparation of Army colors, this flag being smaller than the nearly six-foot-square size required by those specifications.

This fragile silk flag is devoid of color and severely damaged on the fly and bottom white stripe. In the process of conserving the flag, they have been encapsulated to represent the flag's original appearance.

This flag was made for service in the Mexican-American War, during the presidency of James K. Polk. The first U.S. postage stamps were issued in 1846 and the same year the Oregon Treaty drew a border between British and American claims to territory in the Northwest.

GALLERY II

Mexican-American War Commemorative Textile

Date:
About 1848

Size:
78" wide x 94" long

Media:
Cotton fabric (white) and wool (blue) woven textile

Provenance:
Acquired by the Veninga Flag Collection in 1999.
LV01

An inscription by textile maker J.S. Washburn—who may have been from Fall River, Massachusetts—refers to the Declaration of Independence which had been adopted 72 years previously. However, the textile was also made in honor of a recent event—the American victory over Mexico in war. On February 22, 1848, George Washington's birthday, Philadelphia witnessed the "Buena Vista Festival" marking the first anniversary of General Zachary Taylor's success at the Battle of Buena Vista. On June 7, 1848, also in Philadelphia, Taylor was nominated by the Whigs for president and went on to electoral victory that year.

Framing the central floral pattern of the textile are repeated images. A very stylized eagle derived from the U.S. Great Seal alternates with an unidentified domed building. Along the sides of the textile the building is replaced by Masonic symbols. The two pillars with globes at the top are said to symbolize strength and choice. Above appear the traditional compass and square, standing for spirituality and morality. A 19th century Masonic flag showed the compass and square in white on a blue background.

The Flags of the Principal Nations of the World Flag Chart

The principal use of flags during the 18th and the early 19th centuries was to identify the nationality of a ship at sea. To this end, hand-colored charts of the merchant and naval flags of the world's nations were prepared for the use of sea captains. This example, *The Flags of the Principal Nations of the World*, was printed in Philadelphia in 1837 utilizing the copper engraving process. It was then hand-colored for customers willing to pay extra. Note that Texas, shown as a separate nation, is represented by its naval ensign of 13 alternating red and white stripes and a blue canton bearing a single star. The more familiar "Lone Star" Texas national flag, now serving as the Texas state flag, was not adopted until 1839.

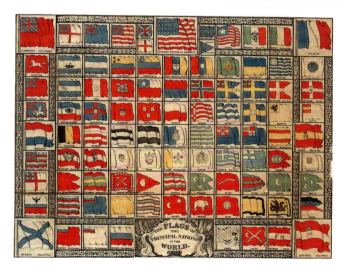

Detail of Texas' ensign

13-Star United States Private Ensign

Contemporary illustrations from the 1780s indicate that the 13 stars of the United States flag of that period were occasionally arranged as a circle of 12 around a single central star. While illustrations suggest that this pattern was "in the public mind" in the 18th century, no documented flag predating the 19th century is known to survive with this star arrangement. The flag attributed to the 3rd Maryland Infantry, supposedly carried by that unit during the Revolutionary War, has been shown to be from a later period. By the 1840s, however, the circular star pattern with a center star began to find favor as a popular manner of displaying 13 stars on patriotic and political flags.

While the use of the U. S. flag today is ubiquitous, during the first half of the 19th century, display of that flag by the general public was limited. Moreover, while government installations were identified by their flying the United States flag, until 1835–1841 the U.S. military did not carry the Stars & Stripes into the field. The small size of this particular flag, combined with the use of three pairs of fabric ties to secure it to a staff suggests that the flag flew from a small boat or yacht of an American family residing on the Atlantic Coast.

(Left)
Date:
1837
Size:
18" wide x 22" long
Media:
Copper engraving with hand coloring
Provenance:
Acquired by the Zaricor Flag Collection in 1995 from a rare book dealer in San Francisco, CA.
ZFC0277

(Right)
Date:
About 1840 – 1860
Size:
21" hoist x 25" fly
Media:
Wool bunting with cotton stars and linen heading; hand-sewn
Provenance:
Acquired by the Zaricor Flag Collection in 2002 from the Mastai Flag Collection through auction at Sotheby's of New York City.
ZFC0609

29-Star United States "Economy Flag"

Date:
1847 – 1848

Size:
12" hoist x 15.5" fly

29 Stars:
July 4, 1847 – July 3, 1848 (Iowa statehood December 28, 1846)

Medium:
Printed cotton

Provenance:
Acquired by the Zaricor Flag Collection in 2002 from the Mastai Flag Collection through auction at Sotheby's of New York City.
ZFC0628

"Economy" and political campaign flags had their origins during the presidential election activities in the fourth decade of the 19th century which pitted Whigs against Democrats. The national election of 1840 saw William Henry Harrison running against the Democratic incumbent, Martin Van Buren. As the issues at stake were lackluster, the Whigs brought personalities into the campaign, vaunting "Old Tippecanoe" (W.H. Harrison) as "the candidate of the common people"—although that was far from the case. The campaign turned into the first media blitz with parades featuring banners and flags replete with slogans and pictures and accompanied by replicas of the log cabin Harrison supposedly had been born in.

By 1840 techniques of printing on silk and cotton had been developed such that campaign and small flags could be obtained a very modest prices. This made them ideal for waving at political rallies and parades in great numbers to attract voters and create excitement. They continued in use in later presidential campaigns and even today constitute a standard fixture in American politics. This specific flag was likely made for the 1848 presidential election, when James K. Polk was replaced by Zachary Taylor.

30-Star United States "Economy Flag"

Date:
1848

Size:
14.5" hoist x 21.5" fly

30 Stars:
*July 4, 1848 – July 3, 1851
(Wisconsin statehood
May 29, 1848)*

Medium:
Printed cotton

Provenance:
*Acquired by the Zaricor Flag
Collection in 1997 from
C. Wesley Cowan of
Cincinnati, OH.*

ZFC1456

The 1848 presidential election campaign saw Democratic Party candidate Lewis Cass pitted against Whig Party candidate Zachary Taylor. Best known for his victory at Buena Vista during the Mexican War, General Taylor achieved success by using the same campaign tactics the Whigs at employed in 1840. The 30-star version of the U.S. national flag played its role in the campaign in the form of numerous inexpensive small flags, probably made by Annin & Co. of New York, a flag business founded in 1847.

These flags both bear the double concentric rings pattern, created when flag manufacturers began to employ methods of accommodating the increasing number of stars.

Three U.S. presidents served under this flag, James K. Polk, Zachary Taylor and Millard Fillmore. During this period the first conventions were held to discuss woman's suffrage and the "California Gold Rush" commenced, enticing thousands to seek their fortune in the West.

GALLERY II

30-Star United States Flag

Date:
1848–1850
Size:
72" hoist x 120" fly
30 Stars:
*July 4, 1848 – July 3, 1851
(Wisconsin statehood
May 29, 1848)*
Medium:
Silk; hand-sewn
Provenance:
Acquired by the Zaricor Flag Collection in 2002 from the Mastai Flag Collection through auction at Sotheby's of New York City.
ZFC0636

A NEW STAR

The Compromise of 1820 called for a careful pairing of free and slaves states in order to maintain parity between North and South in the U.S. Senate. What would prove to be the last balancing act in conformity with that policy was accomplished during the final months of the War with Mexico. Florida and Texas entered the Union as slave states in 1845. Iowa's entry into the Union on December 28, 1846, had paired with Florida's statehood at 14 states each—slave and free. The balance needed to match Texas' entry was accomplished when Wisconsin was admitted into the Union as the 30th state, the 15th free state. That regional equality was to be short-lived. The new territory acquired from Mexico as a result of the war (1846–1848) reopened the controversy with renewed bitterness.

President Zachary Taylor served only 16 months (March 1849–July 1850) before dying of natural causes. Meanwhile, thousands moved to California in the 1849 "Gold Rush." This influx of Americans into California set the stage for statehood and a new crisis over the issue of slavery.

The End of Compromise: Stars Excluded, Stars Defended

"Exclusionary Flags," 1850–1860

"An Alabama steamboat captain has got up an Alabama flag, in the same shape as the usual American flag, but instead of thirty-three stars, he puts one large star in the center, encircled by seven stars, representing the seven principal cotton states."
—*Columbus, GA.* Weekly Sun, *January 22, 1861*

The end of the war between the United States and Mexico netted the United States a large parcel of land that would eventually become all or parts of several southwestern states. That addition of territory, however, raised the question as to whether states formed from it would be "free" or "slave."

The discovery of gold in California in 1849 brought an onrush of new residents to that portion of the "prize" and by 1850 California Territory was clamoring for statehood—as a free state, even though its southern half fell below the 36 degrees, 30 minute demarcation line established as the northernmost border for slave states under the Missouri Compromise.

On September 9, 1850, California was admitted into the Union as its 31st state— but at a cost. As part of a compromise to permit California's entry as a free state, the Old South received a number of concessions that primarily dealt with the capture of runaway slaves.

This "Compromise of 1850" drove a wedge between the North and the South. The admission of California as a free state without the counterbalancing admission of a new slave state began the decline of the power over the U.S. Senate by the South. The decline was further accentuated in 1858 and 1859 when first Minnesota and then Oregon both entered the Union as the 32nd and 33rd states, both "free." Despite these victories, radical abolitionists clamored against the South and in some cases made flags that excluded the 15 slave states, (thus the term exclusionary flags.) Radical abolitionists and pro-slavery secessionists denounced the Union Abraham Lincoln would eventually save.

31-Star United States Mourning Flag

Date:
1850 – 1851
(probably reused in 1865)
Size:
35" hoist x 49" fly
31 Stars:
July 4, 1851 – July 3, 1858
(California statehood September 9, 1850)
Media:
Printed cotton later decorated with black silk crepe border
Provenance:
Acquired by the Zaricor Flag Collection in 1996 from the Star-Spangled Banner Flag House Collection of Baltimore, MD.
ZFC0125

The star arrangement of this Stars & Stripes reflects a frugal modification of an older 30-star flag printing block by the inclusion of an extra star to represent California's admission to the Union. From 1840 through 1860, inexpensive flags were printed on cotton utilizing the same type of carved wooden blocks that were used for printing illustrations. Rather than make an entirely new printing block for a 31-star canton, the craftsman at the flag factory where this flag was produced simply added one star to the original pentagonal design. This saved the labor that would have been required for cutting 31 new stars on a new block. Thus another pattern was added to the existing repertory.

In 1850 President Zachary Taylor died in office—only the second president to do so. (William Henry Harrison, who caught pneumonia during his inauguration address, had died after a month in office in 1841.) In accordance with Victorian-era practice, the border of this flag was decorated with black silk crepe to indicate that its owner was mourning the loss of an important person. According to family tradition, this flag was brought out again in 1865 and displayed in honor of Abraham Lincoln, after he was assassinated in April that year.

GALLERY III

31-Star, 14-Stripe United States Flag

Date:
1851 – 1857

Size:
42.5" hoist x 74" fly

31 Stars:
July 4, 1851 – July 3, 1858 (California statehood September 9, 1850)

Media:
Wool bunting with cotton stars; hand-sewn

Provenance:
Acquired by the Zaricor Flag Collection in 2002 from the Judge John T. Ball Collection of San Jose, CA.
ZFC0585

California was admitted to the Union as a free state according to the terms of the Compromise of 1850 which, instead of pairing each new free state with a new slave state, gave the South political concessions.

Since 31 stars were not readily ordered into neat rows, flag-makers experimented with a number of alternate arrangements. In this flag, the stars are formed into a "Grand Luminary." The pattern was not unique to this flag or to flags made in California, however. One commentator, viewing the ships in New York Harbor in 1857, noted that the Grand Luminary design predominated among ensigns displayed by merchant vessels and on flags flown to advertise the major hotels in the vicinity.

While utilization of the Grand Luminary is unsurprising, the total of 14 stripes is a puzzle. Ever since the Flag Act of 1818, the number of stripes in the United States flag had officially remained unchanged at 13-one for each of the original 13 colonies. For reasons not currently known, the maker of this particular flag added an extra white stripe, thus giving an equal number of red and of white stripes. This flag flew during the presidency of Millard Fillmore.

Pennsylvania-Made Quilt with Large Eagle in Center

Date:
1830 – 1870 or earlier

Size:
78.5" wide x 96" long

Medium:
Cotton fabric

Provenance:
Acquired by the Veninga Flag Collection in 1999.
LV03

Within two frames of charming flowers, this Pennsylvania-made quilt presents a symbol which many viewers probably can identify only as some kind of bird. Inspired by Pennsylvania Dutch motifs, the figure is clearly based on the coat of arms of the United States. (Compare it with the official version appearing in the U.S. great seal, represented on the reverse of a one-dollar bill.) This eagle still has 13 stars and a shield on its breast, but flowers have replaced the olive branch and arrows—symbols of peace and war—and the crest is gone. The colors reflect those of the floral border.

In European heraldry, the eagle was honored as the powerful symbol of the Roman legions and later of the great emperors of Byzantium, Germany, Russia, Austria, Spain, and of France under Napoleon. It was inconceivable that the average citizen in those lands would presume to modify the official form of such an eagle or to use it in a home-made item like a quilt. The freedom of expression Americans have enjoyed since the earliest days of the Republic has not only allowed but actually encouraged this type of folk art.

GALLERY III

13-Star American Commercial (Merchantman's) Jack of the *S.S. Arctic*

(Right)

Date:

About 1850 – 1870

Size:

88" hoist x 105" fly

Media:

Wool bunting with cotton appliqué and overpainted details

Provenance:

Acquired by the Zaricor Flag Collection in 2002 from the Mastai Flag Collection through auction at Sotheby's of New York City.

ZFC0621

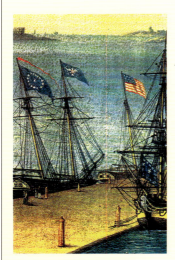

Note the flag usage recorded in this 1802 oil painting of the Salem Massachusetts dockyards, courtesy of the Peabody Essex Museum in Salem, MA.

The Union Flag of Great Britain was established in 1606 to symbolize the joining of the England and Scotland under the common crown of King James I. It was not, however, the main flag of the king's ships but was used as a secondary identifying flag flown from a jack staff positioned at the bow of those ships. In 1634, a proclamation was issued that prohibited all but the Royal Navy from flying the Union Jack at the bow of British ships. In 1674, this restriction was re-emphasized, at the same time that the Red Ensign was established as the official flag of British merchant ships. Nevertheless the prohibition was difficult to enforce and often more honored in the breach than not. Merchant ships continued to illegally utilize the Union Jack initially because it provided several privileges in French and Dutch ports but primarily because it inhibited the impressment of seamen by larger naval vessels. Impressment of seamen would prove a friction point between Britain and the fledgling United States in the first decade of the 18th century.

Unlike English law, nothing in American naval practice prohibited American merchantmen from flying jack flags. Many American merchantmen outfitted their ships with not only the American ensign, but also with a jack flag that copied the canton (union) of the U.S. flag.

Some American commercial flags often incorporated the U.S. coat of arms into the union with the stars. Commercial jacks accordingly complemented their ensigns and similarly bore the U.S. coat of arms.

This commercial jack was used by the ship *Arctic*; however, at least seven commercial vessels carried that name in the period in which this flag dates.

The American Anti-Slavery Almanac for 1844

Page 36 of The American Anti-Slavery Almanac for 1844, *from the Collection of the Flag Research Center, Winchester, MA.*

This verse by William Lloyd Garrison, the editor of The American Anti-Slavery Almanac, *drew early attention to the sectional strife within the nation well before the Civil War. Note the black and white stars on the stylized flag, denoting the northern and southern states as "free" and "slave" states. The slave is bound by the flag's halyard, out of reach of the liberty cap.*

32-Star, 11-Stripe United States Flag

On May 11, 1858, Minnesota Territory advanced to become the 32nd state of the Union. Less than two months later, on July 4, 1858, its star was officially added to the United States flag.

This flag, although homemade, nevertheless is partially machine-sewn, perhaps by one of the recent immigrants from Scandinavia who flooded the territory in the decade between 1848 and 1858. Only 11 stripes compose the field, beginning and ending with a white stripe rather than the more traditional red. The 32 stars are set in diagonal rows that expand from one through seven in number and then descend in reverse order. Those stars are neatly hand-sewn to the blue canton, which rests neither on a red nor a white stripe but overlaps the fifth stripe. The 32-star flag was used only during the presidency of James Buchanan.

17-Star United States Exclusionary Flag

This flag, with its 17 stars, would seem to have been made between Ohio's admission to the Union in 1803 as the 17th state and Louisiana's achievement of statehood in 1812. However, the fact that the stripes and canton of the flag are machine-sewn precludes its having been manufactured before 1850. They suggest that it is, instead, an abolitionist exclusionary flag.

The Fugitive Slave Act—passed as one of the elements of the Compromise of 1850—allowed slave catchers to roam the North in search of anyone who had escaped slavery. The presence of these individuals in New England particularly enraged abolitionist elements there, with some extremists going so far as to advocate Northern secession from the Union rather than submission to the outrages of the Fugitive Slave Act. Exclusionary Stars & Stripes made during the period from 1850 to 1860 reflected that sentiment. Such flags featured stars only for the free states, excluding the 15 slave states from the total represented. This 17-star flag, therefore, is thought to date from around 1858–1859, when 17 free and 15 slave states formed the Union during the presidency of James Buchanan.

(Left)
Date:
1858–1859
Size:
62" hoist x 101" fly
Medium:
Cotton; machine-sewn with hand-sewn stars
Provenance:
Acquired by the Zaricor Flag Collection in in 2002 from the Mastai Flag Collection through auction at Sotheby's of New York City.
ZFC0651

(Right)
Date:
About 1858–1859
Size:
46" hoist x 69" fly
Medium:
Cotton; machine-stitched except for hand-stitched stars
Provenance:
Acquired by the Zaricor Flag Collection in 1996 from the Star-Spangled Banner Flag House Collection of Baltimore, MD.
ZFC0022

33-Star "Grand Luminary" United States Flag

Date:
1859–1861

Size:
68" hoist x 131" fly

Medium:
Cotton; machine-stitched with hand-sewn stars

Provenance:
Acquired by the Zaricor Flag Collection in 1996 from Harry Oswald of Portland, OR.
ZFC1155

As with the 31-star flag, the stars of the 33-star flag did not allow for an orderly arrangement of rows. The alternative "Grand Luminary" star arrangement had been advocated four decades earlier as a star pattern for "civil" U.S. flags, but it still enjoyed great popularity at the beginning of the Civil War, as this homemade flag demonstrates. While it has been suggested that this may have been an earlier U.S. flag with 31 stars, the slightly smaller stars that fall outside the perimeter of the "great star" and that seem to have been added later in fact are made from the same material as the other stars. This suggests that they were all applied at the same time.

In November of 1860, four parties presented candidates for the presidency. Although he did not receive the majority of the popular vote—and was not even on the ballot in nine southern states—Abraham Lincoln was elected president with a majority of the electoral votes.

This flag possibly served during both the James Buchanan and Abraham Lincoln administrations.

18-Star United States Exclusionary Flag

Date:
1860

Size:
30" hoist x 47" fly

Media:
Wool bunting with cotton stars

Provenance:
Acquired by the Zaricor Flag Collection in 2002 from the Mastai Flag Collection through auction at Sotheby's of New York City.

ZFC0630

This flag flew on the ship *United States* when it departed Boston harbor during the James Buchanan presidency in 1860 on the Arctic Expedition led by Dr. Isaac Israel Hayes. Only 18 stars, arranged in two concentric rings around a center star, grace the union of this flag, although 33 stars should have been represented in the canton. Given the Boston origin of the expedition, the makers of this flag excluded stars for the 15 slave states from the union of this flag. During late 1860, rabid secessionists in several Southern states were already applying the same principle in reverse, making United States flags with only 15 stars—one for each of the slave states.

Dr. Hayes returned from the Arctic Expedition and joined the Union Army during the Civil War. Commissioned as a major and assigned as a surgeon to the Sattwell General Hospital in Philadelphia, he was eventually brevetted colonel for his service. He returned to the Arctic once more after the war before settling in New York City, which he represented in the New York State Assembly, until his death in 1881.

32-Star United States Flag, Modified to 34 Stars

Date:
1858 – 1863

Size:
41.5" hoist x 74.5" fly

32 Stars:
July 4, 1858 – July 3, 1859 (Minnesota statehood May 11, 1858)

34 Stars:
July 4, 1861-July 3, 1863 (Kansas statehood January 29, 1861)

Media:
Printed cotton with two additional hand-sewn stars

Provenance:
Acquired by the Zaricor Flag Collection in 1996 from the Star-Spangled Banner Flag House Collection of Baltimore, MD.
ZFC0174

From its construction it is clear that this began as a 32-star flag, honoring Minnesota's entry into the Union on May 11, 1858. The flag became official on July 4th that year, but on February 14, 1859, Oregon was admitted to the Union. While the 32-star flag was official for a whole year, some manufacturers may have anticipated the new 33-star "Oregon flag" by making and selling it before July 4th, 1859.

Because 32-star flags became obsolete after only one year, many probably remained unsold in manufacturers' inventories. Two years after Oregon entered the Union, Kansas was admitted as the 34th state. With the outbreak of the Civil War in April 1861, the demand for 34-star flags quickly outstripped supply. The frugal manufacturer of this printed 32-star flag cut out several stars from other flags of the same style, hand-stitching two of them between the rows to create a 34-star flag to meet consumer demand. Other examples survive of printed 32-star flags modified into the 34-star version. Although firm evidence is lacking, there is reason to believe that these printed cotton U.S. flags may have emanated from Annin & Company of New York City, a firm founded in 1847 and still in existence. Made during the presidency of James Buchanan, this flag was in service during the presidency of Abraham Lincoln.

19-Star United States Exclusionary Flag

Date:
1861

Size:
25.5" hoist x 32" fly

Media:
Wool bunting and cotton stars; machine-stitched with hand-stitched stars

Provenance:
Acquired by the Zaricor Flag Collection in 1996 from the Star-Spangled Banner Flag House Collection of Baltimore, MD.
ZFC0126

Because this flag is machine-sewn it can date to no earlier than 1850, although the 19 stars in its union would lead one to think it was made in honor of the admission of Indiana to the Union in 1816. Its star pattern—14 stars encircling a central one, with an added star in each corner of the canton—was a popular design for the Stars & Stripes from the Mexican War through the Civil War. It is suspected, therefore, that this is an exclusionary flag, made in the North sometime between January 1861—when Kansas was admitted to the Union as the thirty-fourth state—and the February 1861 establishment of the Confederate States of America.

Although the states that formed the Confederacy considered themselves entirely free of the Union upon secession, Abraham Lincoln's administration refused throughout the Civil War to recognize the legitimacy of their putative withdrawal from the United States. While that was the official position of the government, contemporary evidence indicates that a few Northerners did make flags that excluded the seceded slave states.

GALLERY III

33-Star "Eagle in Canton"
U.S. Militia National Color

Date:
1860 – 1861

Size:
76" hoist x 115" fly

33 Stars:
*July 4, 1859 – July 3, 1861
(Oregon statehood
February 14, 1859)*

Media:
Oil paint and gilding on silk

Provenance:
*Acquired by the Zaricor Flag
Collection in 1997 from the
De Young Museum San
Francisco CA Collection
through Butterfield &
Butterfield, SF, CA.*
ZFC0001

THE END OF COMPROMISE

This is one of the few ante-bellum California militia flags to survive. Its silk canton is double-sided. The canton bears 33 silver stars—the only one in the exhibition—around a painted rendition of the United States coat of arms. The practice of combining the national arms and the stars in the canton of a U.S. flag began immediately after the War for Independence and was in continuous, if infrequent, use on militia flags through the Civil War. The same emblems also appeared on flags that the government distributed to Native American Indian tribes in its efforts to obtain Native American Indian loyalty during the first quarter of the 19th century.

This flag, like a number of others, bears a different design on the obverse and reverse of its canton. The obverse is the principal side of a flag, normally the one seen when the staff is to the viewer's left. On the obverse of the canton, the artist, who signed his name "Claveau" as part of the artistic design, also incorporated an inscription in gilt letters. Among the 33 silver stars appears "Ever Green Home Guards No. 2," the nickname the militia company from Santa Clara County, called today Silicon Valley, adopted when they were formed. On the reverse side of the canton, the artist expressed the sentiments of the company's men who were willing to fight for "Settlers' Rights & Union Forever."

Reverse side of canton

Artist's name

7-Star Confederate National Flag (The Stars & Bars)

Date:
1861

Size:
23.5" hoist x 40.5" fly

7 Stars:
March 4, 1861 – May 7, 1861 (Confederacy founded February 22, 1861, by South Carolina, Mississippi, Florida, Alabama, Georgia, Louisiana, and Texas)

Medium:
Cotton; hand-stitched

Provenance:
Acquired by the Zaricor Flag Collection in 1996 from the Star-Spangled Banner Flag House Collection of Baltimore, MD.
ZFC0180

Between December 1860 and February 1861, seven slave states of the South took formal actions to withdraw from the Union. In February 1861 delegates from those states met in Montgomery, Alabama, and formed a new nation, the Confederate States of America. On March 4, 1861, the committee that the Provisional Congress had established to consider a new national flag delivered its report on the designs that they had reviewed.

The committee decided in favor of one remarkably similar to the flag of the United States. It featured three horizontal bars of red-white-red instead of 13 red and white stripes and a blue canton incorporating a circle of stars, one for each state of the new confederation. That design was submitted by Nicola Marschall of Alabama. This new "Stars & Bars" was the ultimate exclusionary flag. Eventually the stars grew to a total of 13 in the union of the Confederate Stars & Bars. In May 1863 the Confederate Congress adopted a new flag, the Stars & Bars having often been confused for the Stars & Stripes. Former U.S. Senator and Secretary of the War, Jefferson Davis, was the first and only president of the Confederate States of America.

16-Star United States Navy Boat Flag

Detail of heading

Date:
1857 – 1861
Size:
38" hoist x 71" fly
Media:
Wool bunting with cotton stars; hand-stitched
Provenance:
Acquired by the Zaricor Flag Collection in 1996 from the Star-Spangled Banner Flag House Collection of Baltimore, MD. Gifted to the Flag House by Col. & Mrs. Jesse J. Hinson of Baltimore in 1966.
ZFC0029

Although this flag bears only 16 stars, it does not date from immediately after 1796 when Tennessee became the Union's 16th state. Rather it is clearly a U.S. Navy boat flag dating from 1857–1861 during the presidency of James Buchanan. It is one of those boat flags of the first pattern adopted, characterized by a reduced complement of stars, as is clear from its design and the NYC (Navy Yard Charlestown) stamped on its heading.

From 1798 through the mid-1850s U.S. Navy ensigns manufactured at navy yards had as many stars as there were states in the Union. By 1855, when the total of the states had grown to 31, it was discovered that the great number of stars in the canton of smaller ensigns, when viewed from a distance, became indeterminate. By at least 1857 authorities at the Charlestown Navy Yard in Boston had resolved this problem by reducing the number of stars to 16 for the 5 authorized boat flag sizes. While it is possible that local abolitionists influenced that decision, it is more likely that practicality and aesthetics induced the flag makers to choose the four rows of four stars each as the star pattern. By 1862, the navy yards were using a different pattern involving only 13 stars.

"Guide on the Colors!"

American Flags in Conflict

"The only commands I gave as we advanced were 'align on the colors! Close upon the colors! Close up on the colors!' The regiment was being so broken up that this order alone could hold the body together. Meanwhile, the colors fell upon the ground several times but were raised again by the heroes of the color-guard."
—*Rufus R. Dawes,* Service with the Sixth Wisconsin Volunteers, *1891, describing events at Gettysburg, July 1, 1863*

Contrary to myth, the United States flag—the Stars & Stripes—was not carried by land forces during the War for American Independence or the War of 1812. For reasons not clear, the basic fighting units of the United States Regular Army were not granted opportunity to carry the Stars & Stripes into combat during the first four decades of the 19th century. Instead, to indicate their nationality, regiments of the U.S. Army carried a "national standard"—a large blue flag bearing the coat of arms of the United States in its center. Finally, in 1834 the four regiments of artillery in the Army were permitted to carry the Stars & Stripes in conjunction with their regimental flags. The nine regiments of infantry of the Army were supposed to obtain the similar privilege the next year, but budgetary constraints prevented the transition until 1841—with some units still not having the new national flags in 1844.

While the Regular Army and most of the state volunteer units entered the War with Mexico with national colors, the 1847 Army Regulations limited their use, so that only the blue regimental colors—the old "national standard"—was to be used in the field. State volunteers often followed suit, especially if supplied by the federal government. With the outbreak of the American Civil War, however, the infrequency of the Stars & Stripes in combat ceased. The War had been initiated by the firing upon the United States flag and the state volunteers that formed the bulk of the Union Army were sent off from their communities with a plethora of flags, nearly always including the Stars & Stripes.

Prang Lithograph *Antietam*

(Left)
Louis Prang's 1887 chromolithograph Antietam *courtesy of the Zaricor Flag Collection, Santa Cruz, CA.*
ZFC0310

(Inset)
1862 – 1864,
black and white carte-de-visite of the Color Sergeant with tattered national colors, 6th Connecticut Infantry. Courtesy of U.S.A. Military Institute, Carlisle Barracks, PA.

Probably more United States flags flew in combat during the American Civil War than any other conflict, but their use was not merely to identify the "nationality" of the combatants. They also served a very functional role. In the smoke and din of battle, these large military colors were often all that could be seen on the battlefield. They provided the focal point for guiding a military unit; if the flag advanced, so did the regiment; if the flag fell back, the unit fell back and rallied upon it. Because these flags were important communication tools, they drew an inordinate amount of hostile fire, as testified by the oft-shredded remains that have been deposited in state houses throughout the North after the Civil War.

35-Star United States National Color

Date:
1863 – 1864

Size:
78" hoist x 78" fly

Media:
Silk with gold-painted stars

Provenance:
Acquired by the Zaricor Flag Collection in 2000 from the Madaus Flag Collection of Cody, WY.
ZFC0402

At the start of the Civil War, the Federal Army was for the most part organized from volunteer regiments recruited by the Northern states. During the first year of the War the states provided all the equipment, including uniforms and flags, for these units. In early 1862, however, the federal government took over responsibility for equipping state volunteers.

To meet the need for a color for each unit, the U.S. Quartermaster Department contracted for flags through each of its regional depots. Surprisingly, each depot had its own pattern to guide the contractors in the production of flags.

While the national colors provided to the New York and Cincinnati Q.M. depots had their stars arranged in horizontal rows, the pattern favored by the Philadelphia Depot arranged the stars in two concentric rings around a central star and filled out the canton with four corner stars. National colors—and the accompanying blue regimental colors—were issued to volunteer units unmarked with regimental designations. Unit commanders were responsible for properly inscribing the center stripes and the scrolls of the flags after receipt. This flag was never marked with its unit designation.

United States Infantry Regimental Color
18th U. S. Regular Infantry

Date:
1863 – 1865

Size:
71" hoist x 75" fly

Media:
Silk; designs painted in oil

Provenance:
Acquired by the Zaricor Flag Collection in 2000 from the Madaus Flag Collection of Cody, WY.
ZFC0407

The design of the regimental color carried by the U.S. Army Infantry can be traced to the 1790s. During the Revolution, Army troops were supposed to carry a pair of colors, one that matched their uniform trim, the other of blue. At first both these colors were decorated with distinctive devices easily recognized by each regiment's enlisted men and officers. After the war, however, the multiplicity of devices was replaced by a common symbol, the coat of arms of the United States. The blue flag with the U.S. arms served the U.S. Army as its "national standard" until the 1830s. Beginning in that decade, troops in the field were finally permitted to carry the Stars & Stripes.

The 18th Regiment of United States Infantry was formed in 1861 as part of Lincoln's expansion of the Army to meet the secession crisis. The 18th served in the "western campaigns" (in Kentucky, Tennessee, and Georgia) during the Civil War. After the War, the 18th was sent West to garrison the Bozeman Trail. It garrisoned Fort Phil Kearny in 1866 during the events leading to the Fetterman Massacre. When Fort Phil Kearny was abandoned, the adjutant of the 18th Infantry took this flag with him and it eventually passed to his descendants.

Quilt with 34-Star United States Flag

Date:
1861–1863

Size:
57" wide x 73.5" long

34 Stars:
*July 4, 1861 – July 3, 1863
(Kansas statehood
January 29, 1861)*

Media:
Silk; printed silk all hand-sewn

Provenance:
Acquired by the Veninga Flag Collection in 1999.

LV80

Patriotic American symbolism in quilts has been expressed in many ways. The national red-white-blue colors; the eagle, shield, and other elements from the Great Seal; stars and stripes in any quantity; symbols such as the Liberty Bell, George Washington, the Statue of Liberty, Uncle Sam, the Liberty Cap, etc.; maps and buildings; as well as mottoes, dates, and slogans are constant themes. The flag itself has been rendered in many ways, but this quilt is unusual for its incorporation of an actual flag in the center.

The plaid and patterned materials used here may have been remnants found in the quilter's sewing basket, but the flag was probably bought especially for this project. The 34 stars of the flag suggest the motivation behind the design: under this banner the North was mustering its forces against the Confederacy in order to preserve the Union. (Kansas, the 34th state, had acquired statehood on January 29, 1861, but some flags made before the 4th of July anticipated statehood by adding a star early.) The quilt thus speaks of Abraham Lincoln's efforts to preserve national unity at a time when it was directly threatened.

34-Star United States National Color St. Louis Home Guard

In 1861 St. Louis, Missouri, was a city divided over the issue of secession from the Union. The southern half of the state, as well as the Missouri River Valley, was dominated by pro-slavery planters. In contrast, after the failed German revolution of 1848 many liberal-thinking Germans had emigrated to St. Louis and the northeastern part of Missouri. Many of those immigrants were staunchly anti-slavery and pro-Union.

When the issue of whether Missouri ought to secede from the Union arose in 1861, the German ethnics of St. Louis organized military units for the city's Home Guard. That force opposed attempts by pro-slavery elements and the governor to organize a State Guard. Led by Captain—later General—Nathaniel Lyon, on May 10, 1861, the St. Louis Home Guard surrounded and captured the camp of the State Guard. While the prisoners were being marched back to St. Louis, a riot broke out. The "Hessians"—as the Home Guard was dubbed by pro-slavery elements—fired into the crowd, killing several. This flag may have served as a regimental or company color for one of the German units involved in the effort to keep Missouri in the Union in 1861.

35-Star United States Flag

West Virginia, the 35th state of the Union, was carved from the mountainous counties of the Commonwealth of Virginia by the pro-Union forces inhabiting that northwestern area of the state. After political machinations to permit the western counties to form a new state from a portion of Virginia (with the constitutionally-requisite consent of both parties), West Virginia was recognized on June 20, 1863 by the United States Congress.

In accord with the 1818 Flag Act, the union of the United States flag was altered to bear 35 stars effective July 4, 1863. Since nothing in that legislation specified how the stars were to be arranged, individuals and manufacturers chose patterns according to their own artistic inspirations. Today many of these designs are treasured as a form of American folk art expressed in cloth.

While a multiplicity of star arrangements characterized the Civil War era, certain regional tendencies arose. In the Mid-Atlantic states, especially Pennsylvania and Maryland, the arranging of the stars in circles and concentric rings tended to predominate. Based on similarities to later flags also emanating from the region, the manufacturer of this flag is thought to have been Jabez W. Loane of Baltimore. (See photo on pages 96–97.)

(Left)
Date: *1861*
Size: *50" hoist x 79.5" fly*
Media: *Wool bunting with cotton stars; all hand-sewn*
Provenance: *Acquired by the Zaricor Flag Collection in 1997 from the De Young Museum San Francisco CA through Butterfield & Butterfield Auctions of S.F., CA.*
ZFC0211

(Right)
Date: *1863 – 1865*
Size: *40" hoist x 67.5" fly*
35 Stars: *July 4, 1863 – July 3, 1865 (West Virginia statehood June 20, 1863)*
Media: *Wool bunting with cotton stars; all hand-sewn*
Provenance: *Acquired by the Zaricor Flag Collection in 1996 from the Star-Spangled Banner Flag House Collection of Baltimore, MD.*
ZFC0023

35-Star United States Recruiting Flag 32nd Indiana Volunteer Infantry

Date:
1864 – 1865

Size:
48" hoist x 108" fly

Media:
Wool bunting with cotton stars; all hand-sewn with painted battle honors

Provenance:
Acquired by the Zaricor Flag Collection in 2000 from the Madaus Flag Collection of Cody, WY.
ZFC0403

Disaster after disaster on the battlefield befell Union armies in 1861 and 1862. These only stiffened the resolve of the Lincoln administration to raise even larger armies to defeat the Confederacy led by Jefferson Davis. As calls went out to the states for "300,000 more," the Quartermaster Department of the Union Army contracted for recruiting flags to stimulate patriotism and increase enlistments for the Union cause. James E. Sebing of New York City was one of the major recipients of Quartermaster

GUIDE ON THE COLORS

Department flag contracts during the War. He made this 35-star recruiting flag under a contract with the New York Clothing Bureau. The flag was subsequently requisitioned by the officers recruiting for the 32nd Indiana Volunteers, then serving in the western theater of the War. The stripes of this flag are decorated with the names of the engagements in which the 32nd had fought, starting with its earliest—Rowlett's Station—and continuing on to Nashville, where a contingent helped break the Confederate siege in December 1864.

Inscribed at the top of the heading is the two line stamp: "J.E. SEBRING Agt. MAKER / 27 Courtland St. N.Y."

United States Army Marking Flag
Company H, 1st N. Y. Veteran Volunteer Engineers

Date:
1865

Size:
18" hoist x 27.5" fly

Media:
Wool bunting, cotton, and wool felt; all hand-sewn

Provenance:
Acquired by the Zaricor Flag Collection in 2000 from the Madaus Flag Collection of Cody, WY.
ZFC0405

At the beginning of the Civil War, the engineer forces of the U.S. Army consisted of a single company of 100 "sappers and miners" stationed in Washington D.C. As the need for the services of this branch became more apparent during the War, a half-dozen engineer regiments were recruited from state volunteers. New York State provided three of these. One was the newly recruited 1st New York Engineer Regiment. In 1864 this volunteer unit "veteranized," i.e. it agreed to continue in service for the balance of the War.

In February 1865 the veteran companies of the 1st New York Engineers received company markers for use when serving as separate units. This is the marking flag of Company H of that regiment. It bears the distinctive branch insignia of engineer troops—a white three-turreted castle—centered on a crimson ground. Yellow scrolls surround it and bear an abbreviated unit name. Superimposed over the castle is a black "H." The 1st New York Volunteer Engineers served in the Department of the South—South Carolina and North Carolina—until 1864, after which it was part of General Benjamin Butler's Army of the James in Virginia.

Civil War Division Headquarters Flag
2nd Division, 9th Army Corps

(Left)
Date:
1864
Size:
45" hoist x 59.5" fly
Media:
Wool bunting and cotton; all hand-sewn
Provenance:
Acquired by the Zaricor Flag Collection in 1998 through James D. Julia Auctions, Fairfield, ME; previously the property of Mr. Courtney Wilson whom acquired it from the Bob Walter Collection of Arlington, Il; who acquired it from Mr. Paul Milikan who originally acquired it from the descendants of General Porter.
ZFC0416

During the Civil War thousands of state volunteers were incorporated into the U.S. Army. The smaller volunteer units were organized into companies, ten of which formed a regiment—the basic fighting unit of the War. Where regiments were concentrated, brigades of two more regiments were formed. In turn brigades were joined to form divisions, while two or more divisions formed an "army corps."

The 9th Army Corps was established in 1862. After service in five Southern states in 1862 and 1863, it returned to Virginia in 1864 under General Ambrose Burnside. During the early months of 1864, the 9th Army Corps fought in the devastating Battles of the Wilderness, Spotsylvania Court House, Cold Harbor, and finally at Petersburg. On July 30, 1864, the 9th Corps was the main Union component in the bloody fiasco of "The Crater." During all these actions the 2nd Division of the 9th Army Corps was commanded by Brigadier General Robert B. Potter.

(Note this flag behind him)

"It Was Go As You Please in the Cavalry"

Louis Prang's 1886 chromolithograph of Sheridan's Ride (Cedar Creek) Courtesy of the Zaricor Flag Collection, Santa Cruz, CA.
ZFC0311

"It is quite possible that General Custer had a different flag before the one in question [his division designating flag]. In the Cavalry especially, they whipped out very fast and had to be replaced."
—J.H. Goulding, Civil War veteran, April 15, 1887

After the War for American Independence, nearly all of the United States Army was disbanded, though trouble on the western frontier soon required the re-establishment of an infantry force. No serious mounted force, however, was formed until 1808 and the units raised then and during the second War with Great Britain were disbanded at the end of that War. Not until 1833 did Congress fund another mounted force—to awe the Plains Indian tribes.

When reformed, the Dragoons—as the cavalry was then called—were authorized a smaller version of the "national standard"—the blue flag decorated with the U.S. coat of arms—as the sole regimental distinction. The Army was in the process of adding the Stars & Stripes to the equipment of each regiment, but funding forced delays until the 1840s, and then the Dragoons were forgotten. While the regimental standard served the Dragoons' needs when the entire unit was assembled together, for the most part cavalry forces served as independent companies or in groups of two companies called squadrons.

For these smaller units, the Army provided "guidons"—literally small flags to "guide upon." From 1833 until 1862, these were cut in the form of a swallowtail and divided horizontally, the top half being red and the bottom half white, with unit markings on both bars.

In 1862, the War Department changed the design of the cavalry guidons so that the swallowtail field was the Stars & Stripes. The many thousands of guidons purchased by the Army during the Civil War served its needs until 1884. The following year the Army went back to the red over white swallowtail pattern for its cavalry guidons and that pattern continues until today. The national flag, the Stars & Stripes, was finally added to the cavalry's regimental inventories in 1895.

During the American Civil War, more cavalry regiments were raised and fought than in any other period of American history. For combat efficiency, these regiments were combined into brigades, divisions, and finally into "cavalry corps" under such famous leaders as Generals Sheridan and Custer. To assist in locating the commanders of these units on the battlefields, both personal flags—which marked the location of a specific individual—and designating flags—which marked the commander of a specific brigade or division—were adopted in the Union Army. Many of these personal and designating flags borrowed from the pre-War traditions of the cavalry.

United States Army Headquarters Flag
2nd Brigade, 4th Division, Wilson's Cavalry Corps

Date:
1864 – 1865

Size:
35" hoist x 54" fly

Media:
Wool bunting and cotton; all hand-sewn

Provenance:
Acquired by the Zaricor Flag Collection in 1998 from the Madaus Flag Collection of Cody, WY.

ZFC0227

During the nearly six months that Brigadier-General James Wilson held the command of the 3rd Cavalry Division of the Army of the Potomac, he had frequent contact with his successor, Brigadier-General George A. Custer, and he undoubtedly saw Custer's personal flag on several occasions. Therefore, it is not surprising that when Wilson sought designs to distinguish the brigade headquarters for the cavalry corps he had been sent West to command in September of 1864 that he chose designs with which he was familiar.

Indeed, all of the "first brigades" of each of his divisions flew flags modeled after the red over white guidon that had marked his own headquarters, while all of the "second brigades" of his divisions followed the designs of Custer's personal flag and thus were red over blue swallowtailed flags. Each of these flags bore the crossed sabers insignia of cavalry, with the addition of the division number in the upper and lower angles of the crossed sabers to distinguish the brigades of one division from another. This particular flag represents the 2nd Brigade, 4th Division, Wilson's Cavalry Corps, and was carried near its commander, Brigadier-General A.J. Alexander, until the close of the War.

United States Army Light Artillery Guidon
Sands' 11th Ohio Battery

Date:
1862

Size:
26.5" hoist x 38.5" fly

Media:
Silk, hand-stitched with painted inscriptions

Provenance:
Acquired by the Zaricor Flag Collection in 2000 from the Madaus Flag Collection of Cody, WY.
ZFC0411

Most of the regular Army's pre-Civil War artillery was known as "foot artillery" because they served in garrisons or forts manning their heavy guns. However, within each of the four artillery regiments of the Army, beginning with the War with Mexico, two companies per regiment were detailed as "light batteries" and were equipped as field artillery so as to be able to accompany infantry on campaign. When the American Civil War broke out, the states furnished large numbers of light artillery batteries for the same purpose. Light—or field—artillery batteries were treated as mounted units since horses drew the guns in the field. Because some of the regular Army field batteries had equipped themselves with the red over white swallowtailed cavalry guidon prior to 1861, many state volunteer batteries formed during the War did so as well. Captain Sands' 11th Ohio Battery of Volunteer Light Artillery was no exception. In 1862 they received this swallowtailed guidon bearing both the unit nickname and two battle honors. At Iuka, Mississippi, in September, Confederate infantry overran and captured Sands' Battery. This guidon, happily, was saved at the time.

United States Army Red Over White Swallowtailed Model 1833 Guidon

Date:
1861
Size:
27" hoist x 41" fly
Media:
Silk; hand-sewn with painted inscriptions
Provenance:
Acquired by the Zaricor Flag Collection in 2000 from the Madaus Flag Collection of Cody, WY.
ZFC0410

Although the War Department did not authorize the Stars & Stripes for regiments of the mounted services of the United States, each company—"troop"—was to carry a small swallowtailed flag to "guide upon"—the folk etymology for "guidon". When Congress reauthorized the formation of a military unit for mounted service in 1833, the pattern of these guidons followed the pennants that were carried on Polish lances, i.e. they were divided horizontally, red over white. The upper red bar was to have the letters U.S. while the lower white bar was to have the company letter.

While the regulations for this pattern did not change until 1862, minor modifications were permitted for practicality.

This is one of the very few Model 1833 cavalry guidons, as modified in 1861, to survive. Nearly 400 were in stock at the end of 1862, when the pattern of the guidon was changed to the Stars & Stripes motif. All were on hand in Philadelphia, the main flag depot at the time, and were distributed to two flag makers for alteration to the new 1862 pattern. This flag survives from that period.

United States Army Regimental Cavalry Standard

Date:
1864

Size:
25.5" hoist x 29.5" fly

Media:
Silk; with coat of arms, scrolls, and stars painted in oil

Provenance:
Acquired by the Zaricor Flag Collection in 2000 from the Madaus Flag Collection of Cody, WY; previously part of the State Fencibles Armory Collection of Philadelphia, PA.
ZFC0412

Due to the expense of maintaining a mounted force, Congress had discontinued the U.S. Cavalry after the War of 1812. In 1833, to awe the Plains Indians into submission, Congress raised a new regiment of "Dragoons." By 1861 the mounted force of the regular U.S. Army had grown to six regiments, each of which carried a single "standard" in place of the national and regimental colors authorized for units serving on foot.

The cavalry standard was a miniaturized version of the old "national standard" of the Army. When mounted forces were reauthorized in 1833, the flags carried by infantry and artillery were undergoing a transition and the Stars & Stripes was gradually becoming standard for the foot forces. For reasons no longer clear, when those forces were finally all furnished with their national colors by the mid-1840s, the mounted forces' need for a similar pair was forgotten. Indeed, until 1895 the blue standard —changed in 1887 to yellow—was the only flag carried when a mounted regiment served together, such as the one shown above from the Civil War. In 1895 the Stars & Stripes was finally granted to each regiment of cavalry.

35-Star United States Army Cavalry Guidon, 1862 Model

Date:
1863 – 1865

Size:
27.5" hoist x 40.5" fly

35 Stars:
July 4, 1863 – July 3, 1865 (West Virginia statehood June 20, 1863)

Media:
Silk with gilt stars; all hand-sewn

Provenance:
Acquired by the Zaricor Flag Collection in 2000 from the Madaus Flag Collection of Cody, WY.
ZFC0409

Although the cavalry of the United States Army was not officially provided with the Stars & Stripes at regimental level until 1895, in January 1862 the War Department changed the pattern of the swallowtailed guidons that were carried by each company ("troop") of a regiment to the design of the Stars & Stripes. More than ten thousand of these "Stars & Stripes guidons" were made and carried during the Civil War. In fact, so many remained after the close of the conflict that they were issued—unchanged as to the number of stars—until 1883. Indeed, the individual troops of Custer's command were still carrying guidons of this pattern when they met their fate at the Little Big Horn in Montana Territory in 1876 and at least five were lost when Custer's battalion was obliterated.

This particular guidon, which served both mounted cavalry companies and light artillery field companies, was either lost in Arkansas or carried by a Union Arkansas volunteer unit from that state during the Civil War.

GALLERY IV

(Top)
Date:
January 25th, 1864
Medium:
Black and white photograph of Brigadier-General George A. Custer wearing a double breasted jacket that he designed and had tailor-made for himself in the Autumn of 1863.
ZFC0750

(Bottom right)
Date:
1861 – 1863
Medium:
Brass and leather
Provenance:
Acquired by the Zaricor Flag Collection in 1995 from the descendants of G. A. Custer, through Butterfield & Butterfield Auction House of San Francisco, CA.
ZFC0492

Brigadier-General George Armstrong Custer

General Custer's speech to the soldiers of the 3rd Cavalry Division, at Appomattox Court House, Virginia, April 9, 1865, after the surrender of Robert E. Lee:

With profound gratitude toward the God of battles, by whose blessings our enemies have been humbled and our arms rendered triumphant, your commanding General avails himself of this, his first opportunity to express to you his admiration of the heroic manner in which you have passed through the series of battles which today resulted in the surrender of the enemy's entire army.

The record established by your indomitable courage is unparalleled in the annals of war. Your prowess has won for you even the respect and admiration of your enemies. During the past six months, although in most instances confronted by superior numbers, you have captured from the enemy, in open battle, one hundred and eleven pieces of field artillery, sixty-five battle-flags, and upwards of ten thousand prisoners of war, including seven general officers. Within the past ten days, and included in the above, you have captured forty-six pieces of field artillery and thirty-seven battle-flags. You have never lost a gun, never lost a color, and have never been defeated; and notwithstanding the numerous engagements in which you have borne a prominent part, including those memorable battles of the Shenandoah, you have captured every piece of artillery which the enemy has dared to open upon you. The near approach of peace renders it improbable that you will again be called upon to undergo the fatigues of the toilsome march or the exposure of the battle-field; but should the assistance of keen blades, wielded by your sturdy arms, be required to hasten the coming of that glorious peace for which we have been so long contending, the General commanding is proudly confident that, in the future as in the past, every demand will meet with a hearty and willing response.

Let us hope that our work is done, and that, blessed with the comforts of peace, we may be permitted to enjoy the pleasures of home and friends. For our comrades who have fallen, let us ever cherish a grateful remembrance. To the wounded and to those who languish in Southern prisons, let our heartfelt sympathy be tendered.

And now, speaking for myself alone, when the war is ended and the task of the historian begins—when those deeds of daring which have rendered the name and fame of the Third Cavalry Division imperishable are inscribed upon the bright pages of our country's history, I only ask that my name be written as that of the commander of the Third Cavalry Division.

G A Custer
—G. A. Custer, Brevet Major General Commanding

Custer's Model 1851 sword belt plate as shown in photo

General George A. Custer's Headquarters Command Flag, 3rd Division, Cavalry Corps

Date:
1864

Size:
41" hoist x 32.5" fly

Media:
Wool bunting and cotton; hand-sewn

Provenance:
Acquired by the Zaricor Flag Collection in 1995 from the descendants of G. A. Custer, through Butterfield & Butterfield Auction House of San Francisco, CA.
ZFC0490

In 1864 when General Sheridan came East with General Grant and assumed command of the Cavalry Corps of the Army of the Potomac, he instituted a special headquarters flag for the commanders of each of his three cavalry divisions. The flag imitated the pre-War cavalry guidon in that it was swallowtailed in form and divided horizontally, red over white. On each of the two horizontal bars, the respective division number was applied in the color of the opposite bar.

The 3rd Cavalry Division of Sheridan's Cavalry Corps was initially commanded by Brigadier-General James Wilson. In September 1864, however, Wilson was transferred to the western theater to command his own cavalry corps (see page 79). Brigadier-General George A. Custer then commanded the 3rd Cavalry Division until the close of the War. Custer (or rather his orderlies; see photo) carried this flag along with his own personally-designed flag in the campaigns that followed, until the 3rd Division flag became too worn out in the last week of the war.

Detail: Orderly with Custer's 3rd Division flag, December 25, 1864

GALLERY IV

General George A. Custer's Third Personal Cavalry Headquarters Guidon

0(Center)

Date:
1864

Size:
32" hoist x 73" fly

Media:
Wool bunting with cotton crossed sabers; all hand-sewn

Provenance:
Acquired by the Zaricor Flag Collection in 1995 from the descendants of G. A. Custer, through Butterfield & Butterfield Auction House of San Francisco, CA.
ZFC0489

(Right)

Date:
1864

Medium:
Black and white photograph by William H. Bowlsby. (See detail of photo on page 85)
ZFC1492

Shortly after receiving his commission as a brigadier-general and closely following the Battle of Gettysburg, George Armstrong Custer caused to be made a swallowtailed guidon, divided horizontally red over blue with white crossed sabers. This served as his personal guidon to mark his location in the field of battle and in camp. The first one was crude, but it was replaced in the Winter of 1863 – 1864 by an elaborate flag of the same design made of silk, fringed, and decorated with battle honors from Custer's 1863 service. In June 1864 this second personal flag was nearly captured; it was saved only by tearing it from its staff. As it was too damaged in the process for further use, in the Summer of 1864 Custer's wife made yet a third personal flag, which was his most famous. This is that very flag.

Custer's third personal flag was carried by him through the remaining campaigns of 1864, including

GUIDE ON THE COLORS

General Custer to his wife Elizabeth (Libbie), opposite White House on the Pamunkey River, March 11, 1865:
"…Well, thanks to the care of a kind Providence, your Bo is safe and well. We will probably cross tomorrow. Meanwhile my command is drawing forage and rations from the loaded vessels in the river. Our raid has been a chain of sucesses, and the 3rd Division has done all the fighting. I wish you could see your boy's headquarters now. My flag is floating over the gate, and near it, ranged along the fences, are 16 battle-flags, captured by the 3rd Division…"
—Custer *by Jeffrey D. Wert (New York: Simon & Schuster, 1996) page 212.*

the Shenandoah Valley campaign, where Custer was photographed with it, and his 3rd Division guidon, in front of his headquarters. It also started with him on the Spring 1865 campaign south of Petersburg and was only replaced by another fine silk example, crafted by his wife, Libbie, as Custer began the final battles on April 1, 1865, that culminated at Appomattox Court House in April 9, 1865.

Major General George A. Custer's Headquarters with his two guidons (see page 85 and above), Winchester, Virginia, December 25, 1864

35-Star United States Flag
Associated with General George H. Thomas

Date:
1864 – 1865

Size:
84" hoist x 138" fly

35 Stars:
*July 4, 1863 – July 3, 1865
(West Virginia statehood
June 20, 1863)*

Media:
*Wool bunting with cotton stars;
all hand-sewn*

Provenance:
*Acquired by the Zaricor Flag Collection in 1996 from the Star-Spangled Banner Flag House Collection of Baltimore, MD.
ZFC0142*

This large 35-star U.S. flag is thought to have flown over the headquarters building of Major General George H. Thomas during the siege of Nashville on December 15 – 16, 1864. At Nashville, General Thomas' forces soundly routed the remains of the Confederate Army of Tennessee in the hills surrounding the important railroad and supply center. Thomas' victory cemented his command over the middle theater of the Union armies.

This flag bears General Thomas' name on at least one of its stars (right). The post-War owner of this flag claimed that it also had flown at Appomattox Court House after General Lee surrendered. However, since General Thomas was still in command of the Department of the Cumberland in Nashville when the surrender took place, that claim makes it likely that Thomas signed this flag after the war. Though evidence is lacking concerning a U.S. flag having been present at the McLean House where Lee's surrender took place, it seems likely, given the number of troops present, that a large camp flag would also have been present at one of the camps occupied by the Union forces.

Detail of General George Thomas' name on a star

36-Star United States Flag Unit Flank Marker

Both the size and the fact that this flag is fringed suggest that it served as a small "flank marker" made to indicate the location of an infantry regiment's flanks when in line of battle or on parade. Although the star representing Nevada's statehood would not officially be added to the canton of the U.S. flag until July 4, 1865, Nevada had become the nation's 36th state eight months earlier and a few flag manufacturers recognized that occasion and added its star to the flags they made in the waning days of the Civil War.

This flag is delicately made with gilt stars, suggesting that it may have been prepared for one of the units participating in the Grand Review of the Union Army which took place in Washington D.C. on May 24–25, 1865, during the presidency of Andrew Johnson. Unfortunately, no record survives of which unit carried it or precisely when or where it was made.

Program for the Restitution of the Stars & Stripes Over Fort Sumter

At 4:30 a.m. on April 12, 1861, Confederate batteries began bombarding the United States flag flying over Fort Sumter in Charleston Harbor, South Carolina. Ultimately that attack led to the fort's surrender at 1:30 p.m. the following day, April 13th, and on the 14th the fort's commander, Major Robert Anderson, was permitted a final salute to his colors and the privilege of keeping his struck flag.

Throughout the Civil War, the recapture of Fort Sumter remained a constant—if elusive—symbolic goal of the Lincoln administration. Months of siege and steady bombardment plus several unsuccessful attempts to take the battered fort by storm all failed, but in February 1865 Charleston was evacuated by Confederate forces. Then the pile of rubble that had been Fort Sumter again came into Union hands. On April 14, 1865, with the Confederacy in its last stages of collapse, elaborate ceremonies were planned for the restoration of the Stars & Stripes on Fort Sumter, as set forth in this program. While those ceremonies did take place, they were overshadowed by the assassination of Abraham Lincoln that occurred that night.

(Left)
Date:
1865
Size:
17.5" hoist x 35" fly
36 Stars:
July 4, 1865 – July 3, 1867 (Nevada statehood October 31, 1864)
Media:
Silk with gilt stars; machine-sewn
Provenance:
Acquired by the Zaricor Flag Collection in 1998 at the J.D. Julia Auction of Fairfield, ME.
ZFC0280

(Right)
Date:
1865
Size:
6.5" x 8.5"
Medium:
Printed paper
Provenance:
Acquired by the Zaricor Flag Collection in 1998 from a rare-book store in Santa Fe, New Mexico.
ZFC0751

GALLERY IV

36-Star "Grand Luminary" United States Mourning Flag

Date:
1865

Size:
26.5" hoist x 36" fly

36 Stars:
*July 4, 1865 – July 3, 1867
(Nevada statehood
October 31, 1864)*

Media:
*Silk with hand-painted stars;
silk crepe border added later*

Provenance:
*Acquired by the Zaricor Flag
Collection in 2002 from the
Mastai Flag Collection
through auction at Sotheby's
of New York City.*
ZFC0617

Although its popularity had waned during the Civil War, the "Grand Luminary" arrangement of the stars to form one great star still found some degree of favor at the end of that conflict. In this small silk flag, 35 small stars are formed into one star surrounding a central enlarged star. All were applied to the light blue silk canton with white paint.

A black silk crepe border was added to this flag during the period of mourning for the death of President Abraham Lincoln. He was assassinated on the evening of April 14, 1865, and died the next morning. As the country mourned, everything from buildings to flags were draped in black crepe, which in Victorian-era parlance symbolized the nation's grief. While most flags were in black silk crepe, some flags with inked black borders also survive.

April 15, 1865 New York Herald *Extra Edition (reproduction 1885), announcing President Lincoln's death. Zaricor Flag Collection (ZFC0324)*

Manifest Destiny: New Stars for a New Land

The Centennial Celebration

"In the east end of the main building at the Centennial Exposition in Philadelphia is a design of the progressive manner in which our national flag was evolved out of the multitude of heraldic suggestions furnished by the American colonies."
—Report on the Main Exposition Building at Philadelphia, 1876

On May 10, 1876, Americans began a six-month celebration of the 100th birthday of United States' independence. From that day until November 9th, exhibits at the Philadelphia Exposition treated the public to the nation's progress in arts and industry. Among the displays in the U.S. War Department gallery was an array of reproduction historic American flags.

Other manufacturers' flags abounded throughout the exhibit hall. Since no star pattern had ever been set by law, each commercial manufacturer arranged the stars in the pattern that it thought artistically pleasing. Moreover, though the official star count at the May opening was 37, most of the flag makers had anticipated Colorado's August 1st entry into the Union and prepared flags bearing 38 stars.

Although only two states were admitted into the Union between 1867 and 1876, in eight months during 1889 and 1890, six more would join the Union. Four joined in November 1889 —North and South Dakota on the 2nd, Montana on the 8th, and Washington on the 11th. And then in July of 1890, two more states were quickly added, Idaho on the 3rd, and Wyoming on the 10th. This sudden adding of states caused havoc among the flag manufacturers of the country. Some makers had produced 39-star flags, others quickly put flags into production with 41 and 42 stars. These were made obsolete when Idaho was admitted a day before the 4th of July. Then the technically official 43-star flag was strangled when Wyoming became the 44th state. The statehood of Utah in 1896 would produce the last change in the 19th century—a flag with 45 stars.

United States Centennial Celebration Flag

Date:
1876

Size:
28" hoist x 47.5" fly

Medium:
Printed cotton

Provenance:
Purchased from Jeff Bridgman in 2002, York County, Pennsylvania. From the collection of Kit Hinrichs.

In celebration of the 100th "birthday" of the Declaration of Independence—and of the United States—one enterprising flag-maker designed and manufactured a special "centennial celebration" flag. These were sold in several sizes during the 1876 exposition at Philadelphia that ran from May of that year through November. The star pattern made no attempt to conform to the proper star-count for the era but instead simply formed the dates 1776 over 1876 across the canton.

Most flag-makers of that era endeavored in their manipulations of the stars to guarantee that the number of stars equaled the number of states currently in the Union. A few anticipated the inclusion of Colorado as the 38th state, during the presidency of Ulysses S. Grant, but some went further, placing 39 stars in the flags that they made for the celebration. These flags anticipated that Dakota Territory would soon enter the Union as a single state, the thirty-ninth. Events would prove those makers wrong.

GALLERY V

(Left)

Date:
About 1870 – 1876

Size:
72" hoist x 97.5" fly

Medium:
Cotton; sewn

Provenance:
Acquired by Kit Hinrichs in 2002 from Kenneth Kohn at the Nashville "Heart of Country Fair."

(Right)

Date:
About 1876 – 1877

Size:
17" hoist x 25" fly

38 Stars:
July 4, 1877 – July 3, 1890 (Colorado statehood August 1, 1876)

Medium:
Printed cotton

Provenance:
Acquired by the Zaricor Flag Collection in 1997 from C. Wesley Cowan of Cincinnati, OH.
ZFC1385

37-Star "American" Flag Junior Mechanics Council (Lodge)

On March 2, 1867, President Andrew Johnson proclaimed Nebraska as the 37th state of the Union. The attainment of statehood had been a lengthy process for Nebraska Territory. It had been created in 1854, but events in Kansas overshadowed attempts by Nebraskans to appeal for statehood until 1864. That year, the Republican-backed statehood bill was blocked by Democrats in the territory.

Finally, in February 1866 the territorial legislature submitted a proposed state constitution to Congress. Because it limited the franchise to whites, that document was returned to the territory. Revised, the Nebraska constitution was resubmitted in February 1867 and approved by Congress, but vetoed by President Johnson. Congress then overrode the veto. Soon after, Nebraska was declared a state.

In 1853, the year before Nebraska Territory was created, the Junior Branch of the Order of American Mechanics had been formed in Germantown, Pennsylvania. This "nativist" (anti-immigrant) organization incorporated separately in 1870 and became an independent organization in 1885. The Order adopted as its corporate symbol the intertwined compass and square of Masonry framing the popular labor symbol of a raised arm bearing a hammer.

38-Star United States Economy Flag

In May 1876, during Ulysses S. Grant's presidency, the United States began the official six-month celebration of the centennial of its Declaration of Independence. The travails of the Civil War were receding into the past and the nation was in a celebratory mood. Flag makers hoped to take advantage of the centennial celebrations. They anticipated Colorado's admission as the 38th state and therefore manufactured 38-star flags well in advance of the official admission of the "Centennial State" on August 1, 1876. That date meant, however, that the 38-star flag would not become official until July 4, 1877.

In printing this small inexpensive "parade" or "economy" flag, the pattern chosen by its manufacturer harked back to the double concentric ring pattern of stars that had been so popular among Mid-Atlantic state flag makers during the Civil War. In this case, however, the stars were arranged in three rings—an inner one of five around the center star, a middle ring of ten, and an outer ring of 20. Two stars were also added to the fly corners of the canton to bring the total to 38. This probably indicates that a printing block originally used for making 36-star flags was modified by adding two stars, even though it resulted in an asymmetrical pattern.

Centennial Exposition Quilt with Flags of All Participating Nations

Date:
About 1876

Size:
89" wide x 91" long

Media:
Printed cotton, muslin

Provenance:
Acquired by the Veninga Flag Collection in 1999.
LV13

Just over a decade after its Civil War, Americans welcomed the opportunity to celebrate the nation and its successes. The great Centennial Exposition held in Philadelphia in 1876 was more than a commemoration of the nation's first hundred years: for visitors from abroad and Americans alike it made a striking statement about the advances the country had achieved in science, industry, commerce, and art. While still largely inward-looking, America was beginning to place greater emphasis on its role in world affairs. This is reflected in the souvenir "flags of the nations" fabric which the quilt-maker perhaps bought during a visit to the Exposition. Several of the designs were inaccurate, but they spoke of the worldliness Americans felt entitled to.

More surprising is the large 39-star Stars & Stripes—a flag which never legally existed. Colorado, the "Centennial State," joined the Union in 1876 as the 38th state, but the next change in the national flag—in 1890—saw five new stars added. It is probable that the mysterious "39th state" was Dakota Territory, whose attempts for statehood were frustrated by internal bickering over its future capital, which eventually resulted in splitting it into two states, thus rendering 39-star flags obsolete.

GALLERY V

38-Star United States Flag

(Center)

Date:

1876 – 1888

Size:

50" hoist x 88" fly

38 Stars:

July 4, 1877 – July 3, 1890 (Colorado statehood August 1, 1876)

Media:

Wool bunting with cotton stars; machine-stitched with hand-sewn stars

Provenance:

Acquired by the Zaricor Flag Collection in 1996 from the Star-Spangled Banner Flag House Collection of Baltimore, MD. ZFC0020

(Far Right)
1864 black and white photograph, courtesy of the Massachusetts Commandry, Military Order of The Loyal Legion and the U.S. Army Military History Institute.

This concentric rings flag is believed to have come from the workshop of flag maker Jabez W. Loane of Baltimore, Maryland. He was active in flag-making in Baltimore from the time of the Civil War through the turn of the century and several flags with the same basic star arrangement have been discovered with a Baltimore association. This design with 35 stars flew upon the train which carried Lincoln's body to Philadelphia.

Loane identified the flags he sold by a code number that referred to their size. In this case the No.10 inked onto the heading refers to a flag that is basically 4.5' along its hoist by 7' along the fly. Loane arranged the 38 stars in two concentric rings around a central star, with 13 stars in the inner ring and 20 in the outer. Four other stars, one in each corner of the canton, bring the total to 38. This flag was so well made that after being rediscovered in 1977 it was carried in the parade for the rededication of Baltimore's City Hall by Mayor William D. Schaefer.

This 1864 view of the "Baltimore Wharf" at Fortress Monroe, Virginia, depicts a 35-star U.S. flag by Jabez Loane, similar to the 38-star version of the same design shown at the left. (See 35-star flag on page 73)

38-Star "Grand Luminary" United States Flag

Date:
About 1876 – 1888

Size:
52" hoist x 92" fly

38 Stars:
July 4, 1877 – July 3, 1890 (Colorado statehood August 1, 1876)

Medium:
Wool; machine-stitched with printed stars

Provenance:
Acquired by the Zaricor Flag Collection in 1994 during a trip to Arkansas and Missouri.
ZFC1423

The 38-star flag was the last commercially-manufactured flag in which the stars were arranged in the form of one great star, the "Grand Luminary" that had originally been proposed by Captain S. C. Reid almost 60 years earlier. He held that it was the form that could best express graphically the concept *E Pluribus Unum*—"Out of Many, One," the national motto. Although the circular or concentric ring pattern would survive another decade, the centennial era essentially brought an end to Reid's insightful and handsome proposal.

The arrangement of the stars in rows had been standard for Navy flags since its rebirth in 1798 and the Army had gradually been won over to the same concept during the Civil War. Nevertheless it would not be until 1912 that all agencies of the federal government would come to follow a common pattern of star arrangement. There is no law that requires the citizens of the country to follow the same pattern.

The 38-star Stars & Stripes flew during the presidencies of Rutherford B. Hayes, James A. Garfield, Chester A. Arthur, Grover Cleveland, and Benjamin Harrison.

38-Star Press-Dyed United States Flag

The heading of this flag bears the inscription "Patent April 26, 1870." This refers to John Holt's improved system for the production of press-dyed United States flags. Although originally patented by Holt, who was from Lowell, Massachusetts, the legal rights were controlled by the United States Bunting Company of the same city, originally founded after the Civil War by General Benjamin Butler.

The United States Bunting Company manufactured numerous flags for both the U.S. Army and the U.S. Navy, but the star patterns used for garrison, storm, and post flags for the Army and for Navy ensigns differed from the arrangement depicted on this flag. It is thought that this flag may have been a product that the U.S. Bunting Company developed for sale to the civilian market during the Centennial celebrations of 1876. Brass grommets, at each end of the white canvas heading, allowed the flag to be attached to a pole or halyard.

In addition to the Centennial Celebration, two other events were celebrated under the 38-star flag. On February 21, 1885, the Washington Monument was dedicated, followed on October 28, 1886, by the unveiling of the Statue of Liberty.

38-Star Press-Dyed United States Flag

The star pattern of this flag conforms to the one stipulated for the "post flag" in the 1889 U.S. Army Quartermaster Department's specifications. However, the official size of the post flag was considerably larger than this flag, which is only 3' by 5'. The post flag was the one normally flown at all Army installations. It was smaller than the garrison flag used on special occasions but larger than a storm flag, hoisted in inclement weather. All three had the same design.

The heading on this flag is marked "Patented Apr. 26th, 1870." This is a reference to John Holt's process for press-dyeing flags, the patent for which was under the control of the United States Bunting Company. That firm may have prepared flags of this star pattern in the hope of interesting other government departments in the purchase of flags with the same star arrangement as was used by the Army. However, that speculation has not yet been documented. Like many details concerning United States national flag history, the facts of the situation may some day be learned from some yet undiscovered archival material.

The population of the country was just over 50 million people in 1880; it had increased to 63 million people by the 1890 census.

(Left)
Date:
About 1876 – 1888
Size:
49.5" hoist x 88" fly
38 Stars:
July 4, 1877 – July 3, 1890
(Colorado statehood
August 1, 1876)
Medium:
Wool bunting; press-dyed
Provenance:
Acquired by the Zaricor Flag Collection in 1996 from the Star-Spangled Banner Flag House Collection of Baltimore, MD.
ZFC0066

(Right)
Date:
About 1880 – 1890
Size:
38" hoist x 62" fly
38 Stars:
July 4, 1877 – July 3, 1890
(Colorado statehood
August 1, 1876)
Media:
Wool bunting; press-dyed
and machine-sewn
Provenance:
Acquired by the Zaricor Flag Collection in 1996 from the Star-Spangled Banner Flag House Collection of Baltimore, MD.
ZFC0012

39-Star United States Flag
"One of the Flags That Never Were"

Date:
About 1876 – 1877

Size:
54" hoist x 86" fly

39 Stars:
Unofficial (Dakota Territory)

Media:
Wool bunting with cotton stars; machine-stitched with hand-stitched stars

Provenance:
Acquired by the Zaricor Flag Collection in 1996 from the Star-Spangled Banner Flag House Collection of Baltimore, MD.
ZFC0038

According to family tradition, this flag was prepared by Mrs. George Kennedy of Philadelphia during the Centennial celebrations of 1876. Mrs. Kennedy not only anticipated that Colorado would be admitted to the Union but that Dakota Territory—then still a single political entity—would enter the Union as well. Her estimation regarding Colorado proved correct.

In Dakota Territory, however, wrangling over the location of the would-be new state's capital prevented the unanimity needed to apply for statehood. During the Centennial celebrations several flag manufacturers, anticipating Dakota Territory's entry into the Union as a single state, produced flags with 39 stars. However, when the territory was finally admitted in November 1889, it had divided into two states. Accordingly there never was an official 39-star U.S. flag.

These flags were first produced during the presidency of Ulysses S. Grant and were used during the administrations of Rutherford B. Hayes, Chester A. Arthur, Grover Cleveland and Benjamin Harrison.

40-Star United States Flag
Unofficial

Before Dakota Territory was finally admitted into the Union, it was split into two separate states—North Dakota and South Dakota. Both were officially admitted on November 2, 1889, as the 39th and 40th states.

However, the number of states changed rapidly that year and the next. On November 8, 1889, Montana Territory was admitted as the 41st state; three days later it was followed by Washington as the 42nd state. Then the day before the 42-star flag would have become official, July 3, 1890, Idaho officially became a state. As a result, the 43-star flag became official the next day. The problem was that flag manufacturers had not anticipated Idaho statehood. This flag, one of a pair, was displayed on a pole from a schoolhouse.

Benjamin Harrison, who was president at the time this flag was used, was one of the first American chief executives to speak publicly in favor of displaying the Stars & Stripes in a dignified manner.

41-Star United States Flag
Uncut Printed Run of Six Parade Flags

The 41st state to enter the Union, Montana, joined on November 8, 1889. Nevertheless it was only three days later that Washington became the 42nd state on November 11. At least one flag maker anticipated that Washington statehood would not become official until after the following July, when the flag would officially change. That anticipation was ill-founded and perhaps it was for that reason that this printed run of flags was never cut and mounted.

(Left)
Date:
1889
Size:
31" hoist x 46" fly
40 Stars:
Unofficial (South Dakota statehood November 2, 1889)
Medium:
Wool bunting; machine-stitched with printed stars
Provenance:
Acquired by the Zaricor Flag Collection in 1996 from the Star-Spangled Banner Flag House Collection of Baltimore, MD. ZFC0024

(Right)
Date:
1889
Size:
16.5" (each) hoist x 23.5" fly
41 Stars:
Unofficial (Montana statehood November 8, 1889)
Medium:
Printed cotton
Provenance:
Acquired by the Zaricor Flag Collection in 1996 from the Star-Spangled Banner Flag House Collection of Baltimore, MD. ZFC0162

41-Star Flag Hat and Apron
(Flag Derivatives)

(Left)
Date:
1889 – 1890
Size:
8.5" x 10.5"
41 Stars:
Unofficial (Montana statehood November 8, 1889)
Medium:
Cotton with printed stars; machine-sewn
Provenance:
Acquired by the Zaricor Flag Collection in 1997 from C. Wesley Cowan of Cincinnati, OH.
ZFC1380

(Right)
Date:
1889 – 1890
Size:
24" hoist x 24" fly
41 Stars:
Unofficial (Montana statehood November 8, 1889)
Medium:
Cotton with printed stars; machine-sewn
Provenance:
Acquired by the Zaricor Flag Collection in 1997 from C. Wesley Cowan of Cincinnati, OH.
ZFC1381

Flag derivatives are non-flag items that incorporate the symbols and/or colors of the United States flag (or portions thereof). They are not intended to be flown from a staff, but still evoke the same general patriotic response that the flag elicits. Such items became common in American folk culture, especially during the last quarter of the 19th century. This hat and apron are but two of among dozens of possible examples of such derivatives from the period 1889 – 1890. They were quite possibly produced for use in one of the 1890 Congressional races.

Widespread, occasionally humorous, use of the flag, especially in advertising commercial products led Congress, by 1890, to consider restrictions to prohibit such "desecration." On February 20, 1905 a Public Law prohibiting use of the U.S. flag and other national symbols in trademarks was adopted.

The use of the flag in fashion, though not prohibited by this legislation, diminished but did not disappear entirely during the first half of the 20th century. However, during the last four decades of that century flag fashion re-emerged as a powerful statement of popular fashion. Cultural self-expression and popular fashion are protected by the Constitution.

"Wearing of the Flag"

The daughter of "Major" William Logan at the Fort Belknap Indian Agency, Montana, bedecked for the 4th of July, 1905 or 1906.

1905 – 1906
Black and white photograph, Courtesy of Sumner Mattison Collection, Milwaukee Public Museum, Milwaukee, Wisconsin.

42-Star United States Flag
Unofficial

Date:
1889 – 1890

Size:
57" hoist x 75" fly

42 Stars:
Unofficial (Washington statehood November 11, 1889)

Media:
Wool bunting and cotton; machine-stitched

Provenance:
Acquired by the Zaricor Flag Collection in 2002 from the collection of Judge John T. Ball of San Jose, CA.
ZFC0595

On November 11, 1889, just three days after Montana was admitted to the Union, Washington Territory followed, becoming the 42nd state. For several months it appeared that there would be no further changes in the star count of the new flag, which was to become official on July 4, 1890. Several flag makers prepared 42-star flags in anticipation of the four new states. Then on July 3, 1890, Idaho was admitted to the Union—only one day shy of the official change date. Suddenly the 42-star flags that had been manufactured in anticipation of Independence Day celebrations were obsolete without ever having been official. This particular flag was handmade by Quakers, during the presidency of Benjamin Harrison. Its star pattern weaves between an organized beginning and a chaotic ending.

43-Star United States Flag

Date:
1890

Size:
50" hoist x 66" fly

43 Stars:
July 4, 1890 – July 3 1891 (statehood: North Dakota November 2, 1889; South Dakota November 2, 1889; Montana November 8, 1889; Washington November 11, 1889; Idaho July 3, 1890)

Medium:
Cotton; machine-stitched

Provenance:
Acquired by the Zaricor Flag Collection in 2002 from the collection of Judge John T. Ball of San Jose, CA.

ZFC0596

The 43-star flag officially heralded the multiple admissions to statehood from the Great Plains and Rocky Mountain area on July 4, 1890, the day after Idaho joined the Union. Although that flag was official for the entire next year, another new state quickly inhibited the manufacture of 43-star flags: only a week after Idaho's admission, Wyoming became the 44th state.

While a star for Wyoming would not become official in the canton of the United States flag for another year, both flag makers and the general populace knew that the 43-star flag would be obsolete shortly. Manufacturers quickly discontinued producing a flag that the public was not prepared to buy. As a result, the 43-star flag is today one of the rarer versions of the Stars & Stripes to be commercially made. This short-lived flag saw service briefly under the presidency of Benjamin Harrison.

GALLERY V

44-Star United States Flag Concentric Ring Pattern

Date:
1891 – 1895

Size:
26.5" hoist x 44" fly

44 Stars:
*July 4, 1891 – July 3, 1896
(Wyoming statehood
July 10, 1890)*

Medium:
Printed cotton

Provenance:
*Acquired by the Zaricor Flag
Collection in 2002 from the
collection of Judge John T. Ball
of San Jose, CA.*
ZFC0597

44 STARS – 22nd FLAG
WYOMING: JULY 4, 1891 – JULY 3, 1896

This flag displays its stars in three concentric rings around a center star of the same size. The inner ring bears six stars, the middle ring twelve, and the outer ring 21. Four other stars, one in each corner, bring the total to 44 stars. The concentric ring pattern dates to the Mexican War. Later, during the Civil War, Philadelphia flag contractors submitted flags of that star pattern to the Army's Quartermaster Department.

The concentric rings appeared first on the swallow-tailed guidons that had been reworked from old stock and then on the national colors provided under contract. At least one Baltimore maker followed suit and continued to make such flags at least into the third quarter of the 19th century. The maker of these well-printed flags is not yet known. Its design is one of the latest known use of the concentric rings star pattern in the U.S. flag design, which represents the end of an era of the use of the stars in a circular constellation.

Under the 44-star Stars & Stripes, Benjamin Harrison finished his term of office as president and Grover Cleveland served in the White House for his second, non-consecutive, term.

45-Star United States Flag

Date:
1896 – 1908

Size:
32.5" hoist x 46" fly

45 Stars:
July 4, 1896 – July 3, 1908 (Utah statehood January 4, 1896)

Medium:
Printed silk

Provenance:
Acquired by the Zaricor Flag Collection in 1996 from the Star-Spangled Banner Flag House Collection of Baltimore, MD.
ZFC0030

On July 4, 1896, following Utah's entry into the Union as its 45th state six months before, America's 45-star flag became official. That flag graced the ships of the country's new steel navy that two years later was to engage Spanish fleets in the Caribbean Sea and in Pacific Ocean at Manila Harbor. It would be carried by the regular army and the volunteers who served in the brief land campaigns of the Spanish-American War in Cuba, Puerto Rico, and the Philippines.

The flag of 45 stars was also involved in peaceful international contacts between the United States and the other major powers of the world. Beginning at the turn of the 20th century and over the next decade, for example, numerous international expositions were held throughout the world and in the United States. The Stars & Stripes was widely displayed and many, purchased by private individuals, were made in decorative silk like this well preserved example.

The United States acquired American Samoa, Guam, Hawaii, Palmyra Island, the Philippines, Puerto Rico, and Wake Island under the 45-star flag, which saw service during the presidencies of Grover Cleveland, William McKinley and Theodore Roosevelt.

United States Army "Model 1885" Cavalry Guidon
Troop F, 11th U.S. Cavalry

Date:
About 1898

Size:
27" hoist x 37" fly

Media:
Wool bunting with cotton inscriptions; machine sewn

Provenance:
Acquired by the Zaricor Flag Collection in 1997 from the De Young Museum San Francisco CA Collection through Butterfield & Butterfield Auctions of San Francisco, CA.
ZFC0210

In 1885, the U.S. Army changed the pattern of the guidon that was carried by the companies—troops—of cavalry regiments. The new pattern reverted to the basic design used by the mounted forces of the Army between 1833 and 1862 and consisted of a swallow-tailed field divided horizontally, red over white. The upper bar bore the cavalry regiment's seniority number, while the lower bar bore the troop letter. At first provided only in silk, in 1890 a "field guidon" of more durable bunting was provided.

This particular guidon was carried during the Spanish-American War and the Philippine Insurrection following the occupation of the Philippines by U. S. forces. Company F, 11th U.S. Cavalry, was serving as the headquarters escort to General Henry Ware Lawton when he was killed at Station San Mateo in Manila on December 19, 1899. This guidon was subsequently sent to California, where it was auctioned to support the Red Cross on June 27, 1917 in San Francisco, to raise funds to aid American soldiers destined for France during World War I.

An interesting footnote—the American Indian Geronimo surrendered to General Lawton in the late 1880s.

GALLERY V

Royal Hawaiian Flag Quilt (Top)

Date:
Late 19th – early 20th century

Size:
80" wide x 82" long

Medium:
Cotton fabric (unfinished quilt)

Provenance:
Acquired by the Veninga Flag Collection in 1999.
LV84

In the late 18th century British and American ships brought to Hawaii the first national flags seen there. In 1816 the first Hawaiian ship to sail abroad hoisted the country's new civil ensign. It consisted of horizontal stripes of red, white, and blue with the Union Jack in the canton—a combination of American and British symbols. Hawaiians became very attached to that flag and mourned its loss when British troops occupied Hawaii in 1843 and again when American settlers overthrew their monarchy in 1893.

This quilt top was probably made in Hawaii after Liliuokalani, deposed as queen, continued to serve as the spiritual leader of Hawaiians (1893 – 1917).

The four modified Hawaiian flags forming the border of the quilt top are referred to by the motto on the red ribbon—*Kuu Hae Aloha*, "Our Beloved Flag."

Also in the center is the royal coat of arms, showing crown and mantling at the top above a quartered shield. The first and fourth quarters bear the flag stripes while the golden second and third quarters feature a *puloulou*, a staff bearing a white ball which had been set at the doors of the king's house as a symbol of sanctuary. Note the error in the bottom Union Jack. Quilt makers commonly inserted "errors" in their work to assert that "only God is perfect."

Trapunto with U.S. Symbols

A "trapunto" is an ornately embroidered commemorative fabric. The trapunto technique consists of adding padding behind a piece of silk to which elaborate designs are embroidered to form a three-dimensional image. Patriotic symbols were a common theme for such items. Many were made and sold by the George Washington Co. in Yokohama, Japan, in late 19th and early decades of the 20th century. Their market included visiting naval officers and men from America's "Great White Fleet," which was circumnavigating the globe to "show the flag" to foreign countries.

Two fierce-looking dragons appear in this trapunto composition below. The fact that one is being attacked by the eagle suggests that this particular trapunto may date from 1900 or shortly thereafter. That year the United States—with other countries—suppressed the Chinese militant secret society, known as "Boxers." This was known as the Boxer Rebellion which occurred during the presidency of William McKinley.

Trapunto with Portrait

The young soldier who commissioned the commemorative trapunto above had a tintype portrait of himself in uniform centered below the U.S. eagle. His portrait is surrounded by a panoply of the flags of the nations that had economic or imperial interests in the area. On the left are the flags of Great Britain (merchant flag), Germany, Spain, Sweden, and imperial China. On the right are the flags of the United States, Italy, Greece, Norway, and Japan. Embroidered surrounding the central panoply are the names of the countries visited—Philippines, China, and Japan. This piece dates from the presidency of William Howard Taft.

(Left)
Date:
About 1900–1910
Size:
24" wide x 34" long
Medium:
Silk; hand-sewn
Provenance:
Acquired by the Zaricor Flag Collection in 1996 from the Star-Spangled Banner Flag House Collection of Baltimore, MD which acquired it in 1989 through Marion Butterwick from Verna Pearthree (deceased.)
ZFC0150

(Right)
Date:
About 1907–1912
Size:
12" wide x 15" long
Medium:
Cotton with silk and metallic embroidery; ferrotype on sheet iron
Provenance:
Acquired by the Veninga Flag Collection in 1998.
LV91 / ZFC0742

A Symbol of World Power: the Stars & Stripes at Home and Abroad

An Equal Among the World's Powers

"It [the "Stars & Stripes] is found in every land, and on every sea, where the foot of man has been. And there is no nation who dares to offer it insult. The haughtiest sovereigns dare not refuse to salute its free folds as it passes by their strongholds of power."
—*Nellie C. Saylor, "Stars and Stripes," 1876*

As the 20th century neared, a new international power emerged. The United States Navy constructed "The Great White Fleet" that the U.S. government would use as an instrument of diplomacy—its "big stick," as expressed by President Theodore Roosevelt. The U.S. exercised that power to overwhelm the navy of Spain in a short yet decisive war with that country in 1898. By the first decade of the 20th century, American naval power had brought the country new international respect and the weight of an "empire."

In the first dozen years of the 20th century, the nation at home also grew. Three new states were added to the Union. The former "Indian Territory" became the state of Oklahoma on November 16, 1907—and its 46th star was recognized in the union of the flag in July of 1908. Then in early 1912, New Mexico and Arizona, the last of the territories of the contiguous United States became respectively the 47th and 48th states on January 6th and February 14th of that year.

The flag of the United States officially changed to 48 stars on July 4, 1912. Four months later, President Howard Taft issued an Executive Order that finally set the star arrangement and the proportions for all of the United States flags purchased by government agencies. This trend to uniformity in the star arrangement had been evolving for the past 20 years within government agencies.

In 1959, respectively January 3rd and August 21st, two new states, Alaska and Hawaii, were admitted to the Union, necessitating two new flags—the 49-star and the 50-star Stars & Stripes—official on July 4, 1959, and July 4, 1960.

United States "Human Flag"

1917 black and white photograph by Maynart Studio, Chicago. Purchased in 1999 at the "Cowboy and Indian" Show in Albuquerque, NM. Courtesy of Kit Hinrichs.

This "Human Flag" was formed in 1917 by 10,000 officers, enlisted ratings and recruits of the U.S. Naval Training Station at Great Lakes, Illinois. These World War I era displays were a popular patriotic practice. The Stars & Stripes effect was created, not by distinctive red, white and blue apparel, but by simply alternating white summer and blue winter uniforms. Since color film was still in the future, such color optical illusions were possible.

GALLERY VI

46-Star United States Flag

Date:
1908–1911

Size:
42" hoist x 78" fly

46 Stars:
*July 4, 1908 – July 3, 1912
(Oklahoma statehood November 16, 1907)*

Media:
*Wool bunting and cotton;
machine-sewn*

Provenance:
Acquired by the Zaricor Flag Collection in 2002 from the collection of Judge John T. Ball of San Jose, CA.
ZFC0599

On November 16, 1907, Oklahoma became the 46th state of the Union. The former Indian Territory had applied for admission as the State of Sequoyah, but Congress rejected it. Subsequently, Oklahoma Territory and Indian Territory joined to frame a new constitution, successfully applying for statehood as the State of Oklahoma.

On July 4, 1908, in accordance with the provisions of the 1818 flag act, Oklahoma's star joined the canton of the United States flag. That was the 23rd official change in the Stars & Stripes since the first one had been authorized in 1777. Four years later the national flag would change again.

Although the Indian Territory never achieved statehood, the U.S. government currently officially recognizes limited rights of sovereignty for over a hundred Native American tribes. Their flags rank after state flags according to official protocol. Both Theodore Roosevelt and William Howard Taft were president under the 46-star U.S. flag.

47-Star United States Flag
Unofficial

Date:
1912

Size:
40" hoist x 64" fly

47 Stars:
Unofficial (New Mexico statehood January 6, 1912)

Media:
Wool bunting and cotton; machine-sewn

Provenance:
Acquired by the Zaricor Flag Collection in 2002 from the collection of Judge John T. Ball of San Jose, CA.
ZFC0600

On January 6, 1912, New Mexico became the 47th state admitted into the Union. No official 47-star flag ever existed, however, because Arizona entered the Union as the 48th state on February 14 of the same year. The official changes to the flag on July 4, 1912 simultaneously recognized both admissions with its total of 48 stars.

Evidently at least one major flag manufacturer had prepared 47-star flags, perhaps in anticipation that Arizona's admission would be delayed, as illustrated by this example. At one point it was anticipated that Arizona and New Mexico might enter the Union as a single state. Because they were unofficial and only produced briefly, 47-star flags are quite rare. This flag was made during the presidency of William H. Taft.

48-Star United States Flag with Staggered Rows

Date:
1912

Size:
14.5" hoist x 20" fly

48 Stars:
July 4, 1912 – July 3, 1959 (statehood: New Mexico January 6, 1912; Arizona February 14, 1912)

Medium:
Printed cotton

Provenance:
Acquired by the Zaricor Flag Collection in 2002 from the collection of Judge John T. Ball of San Jose, CA.
ZFC0601

Several different star arrangements for the 48-star flag were considered in 1912. However, on June 24 that year President William Howard Taft promulgated an executive order that for the first time established an exact star pattern and detailed flag proportions for the newly-changed United States flag. Another executive order, issued on October 29, 1912, specified the size and relative positioning of each star.

Those executive orders were applicable only to government agencies, however. Nothing prevented flag manufacturers from catering to clients outside the government by designing and making U.S. flags according to their own fancy, as in the past. This flag is an example of that continuing trend.

The 48-star flag was used under Presidents William Howard Taft, Woodrow Wilson, Warren G. Harding, Calvin Coolidge, Herbert C. Hoover, Franklin D. Roosevelt, Harry S Truman, and Dwight D. Eisenhower. Although the "staggered row" 48-star U.S. flag was only in use for the first few years after its inception, the 48 star flag itself remained the flag of the land for the 47 years between 1912 and 1959. That record, however, will be broken if the current 50-star U.S. flag remains unchanged beyond 2007.

48-Star United States Peace Flag

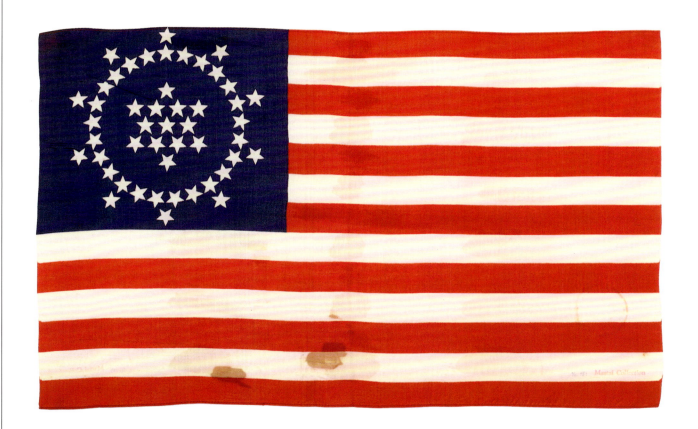

Date:
About 1912 – 1914

Size:
16" hoist x 24" fly

48 Stars:
July 4, 1912 – July 3, 1959 (statehood: New Mexico January 6, 1912; Arizona February 14, 1912)

Medium:
Printed silk

Provenance:
Acquired by the Zaricor Flag Collection in 2002 from the Mastai Flag Collection through auction at South Bay Auction of New York City.
ZFC0635

As early as 1910 Wayne Whipple of Philadelphia, Pennsylvania, started making and promoting his design for a United States flag of 46 stars. It had a distinctive star arrangement indicating that its owner favored peace throughout the world. The pattern that Whipple chose was not unlike some of the concentric ring designs for star patterns that had been common during the Civil War. In Whipple's design the 13 original states are represented by a "great 6-pointed star" in the center of the canton, reminiscent of the pattern displayed over the eagle's head in the coat of arms of the United States. This grouping is surrounded by a circle of 25 stars, representing the states admitted from 1791 to 1876.

The eight other stars—in pairs in each corner of the canton—represented the states that joined the Union after 1876. Two years later, Whipple added two more stars to his design, arranging the now ten stars to represent the states that had joined the Union since 1876 in a circle around the inner ring of 25. Though Whipple would continue to advocate his "flag of Peace" for years, only a few flags were made in accordance with his plan.

GALLERY VI

United States Army 1904 Model Regimental Color 75th U.S. Infantry

Date:
About 1918

Size:
62" hoist x 76" fly

Medium:
Embroidery on silk

Provenance:
Acquired by the Zaricor Flag Collection in 1995 from the U.S. Army Ranger Museum Collection of New York City.
ZFC1439

A SYMBOL OF WORLD POWER

Throughout the 19th century, each infantry regiment of the U. S. Army had continued to carry a blue flag with a version of the coat of arms of the United States applied to its center. Until 1904 the form of the eagle in the coat of arms was a very informal and realistic-looking eagle. The Army then adopted a new rendition for the arms. Instead of a free-flying eagle, the new pattern took on the highly stylized European-type heraldic eagle that continues to serve today.

During the 19th century, the U.S. Quartermaster's Department had great difficulty securing adequate embroiderers to work the emblems on the flags it required. Instead, oil-painted renditions of the arms were often provided as substitutes. When the Army entered the 20th century, the regulations for embroidered devices were enforced. This color was specifically embroidered for the 75th United States Infantry, which was attached to the 13th Division during World War I.

Although the country was generally enthusiastic about entering World War I under President Woodrow Wilson, by the end of his term (1913–1921) he was unable to rally political or popular support for the League of Nations which he believed would help preserve peace.

Detail of hand knitted fringe

U.S. Army "Model 1886" Artillery Guidon
Battery E, 308th U.S. Field Artillery

Date:
1917–1918
Size:
27" hoist x 40" fly
Medium:
Wool bunting with cotton inscriptions; machine-sewn
Provenance:
Acquired by the Zaricor Flag Collection in 1997 from the Baltimore Antique Gun Show, Baltimore, MD.
ZFC0267

Until 1886 the light artillery—field artillery—companies of the U.S. Army had traditionally used the same guidons in field maneuvers as the cavalry. Beginning that year, the artillery was provided with new regimental flags and battery guidons that matched their branch color. Those flags were red and bore the traditional crossed cannon insignia of the artillery. The guidon was completed by addition of the regimental number and the battery letter, the latter below and the former above the crossed cannons.

The 308th was part of the National Army formed during World War One. It was raised in New York, New Jersey, and areas of Pennsylvania adjacent to them as a part of the 78th Division. The 78th was nicknamed the "Lightning Division" by the French, because the battlefield looked as if it had been struck by lightning after they fought there.

48-Star Flag
Franco-Anglo-American Alliance "Humanity Flag"

In 1917 the United States entered World War I on the side of the beleaguered Allied Powers—a failing Russian regime, Britain, and France. To reflect the new alliance between the Americans, British, and French on the Western Front, Albert Hewitt of Mount Vernon, New York, patented this special variation of the United States' Stars & Stripes on February 26, 1918. In his "alliance flag," Hewitt substituted rows of British Union flags for the red stripes of the American flag. The canton, instead of being all blue, was divided vertically into the French Tricolor of blue, white, and red. The 48 stars on that canton are shown in colors contrasting to the Tricolor's bars. Hewitt dubbed his design "the Humanity Flag" because, as he explained, "This flag will make the world safe for Democracy and Humanity."

(Left)
Date:
1918
Size:
11.75" hoist x 17" fly
Media:
Printed silk
Provenance:
Acquired by the Zaricor Flag Collection in 2002 from the Mastai Flag Collection through auction at South Bay Auction of New York City.
ZFC0641

(Inset)
Date:
1918
Size:
16" high x 19.5" wide
Medium:
Oil painting
Provenance:
Acquired by the Zaricor Flag Collection in 2002 from the Mastai Flag Collection through auction at South Bay Auction of New York City.
ZFC0642

GALLERY VI

48-Star United States Flag for Promotion of War Bonds

Date:
1942

Size:
30" hoist x 57" fly

Media:
Cotton bunting with cotton stars, machine-sewn; lettering stenciled in black paint

Provenance:
Acquired by Kit Hinrichs in 1997 at the San Francisco, CA "Cow Palace Antiques Fair."

A SYMBOL OF WORLD POWER

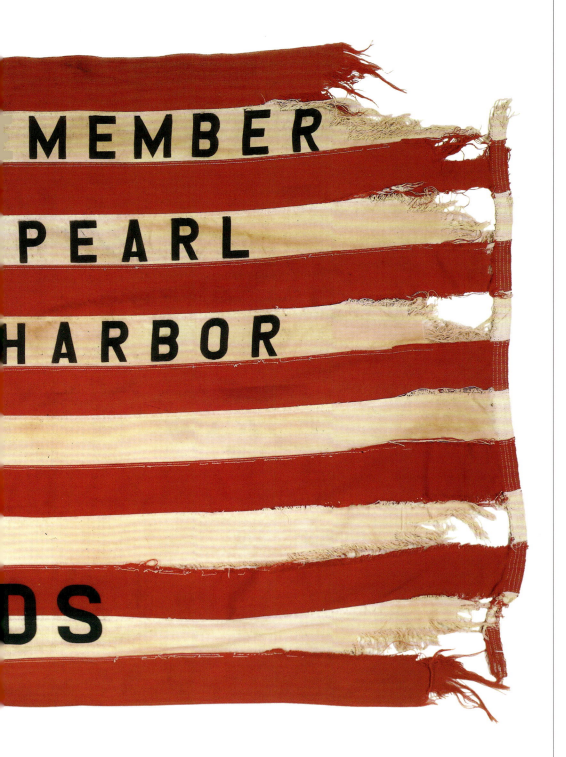

On December 7, 1941, the Japanese Navy unleashed an aerial bombardment of the United States Navy's Pacific Fleet at Pearl Harbor, as well as attacks on other American installations in the Pacific. The attack caught the Navy's and Hawaii's other defenses by complete surprise. The mainstays of the U.S. fleet were destroyed or seriously damaged, with the exception of the aircraft carriers which were then out to sea on maneuvers. President Franklin D. Roosevelt declared December 7th a "day of infamy." The battle cry of the nation, reminiscent of Sam Houston's "Remember the Alamo" cry at San Jacinto, became "Remember Pearl Harbor."

To raise revenue for underwriting the American war effort, the Treasury Department—as it had done in World War I—authorized the issue of war bonds. To mobilize the citizenry behind these efforts much patriotic propaganda was put into circulation. While posters were a more prominent mainstay of this campaign, a number of United States flags were inscribed in black lettering with the joint slogans "Remember Pearl Harbor" and "Buy War Bonds."

On June 22, 1942, Congress adopted in modified form the 1923–1924 recommendations of the National Americanization Commission of the American Legion regarding flag etiquette. Among the rules set forth was a prohibition of inscriptions placed directly on the flag of the United States. Nevertheless this flag saw service at Hickman Field (Hawaii) through much of 1942.

The heading of this flag indicates it was made from "Bull Dog Bunting," a tradename that the Dettra Flag Company employed to distinguish its cotton bunting.

United States Navy Jack, U.S.S. Phelps
First U.S. Flag to Fly Over Japanese Territory in WWII

Date:
1942 – 1947

Size:
35" hoist x 50" fly

48 Stars:
July 4, 1912 – July 3, 1959 (statehood: New Mexico January 6, 1912; Arizona February 14, 1912)

Media:
Wool bunting and cotton; machine-sewn

Provenance:
Acquired by the Zaricor Flag Collection in 1997 from the collection of the late Calvin Bullock of New York City. Acquired by Mr. Bullock from Royal Navy Commander Anthony Kimmins in 1944.
ZFC1083

Detail of heading

The destroyer *U.S.S. Phelps* was in Pearl Harbor, Hawaii, when the Japanese attacked on December 7, 1941. During the ensuing engagement, the *Phelps* was credited with downing at least one Japanese plane and with assisting in the destruction of three others. After the battle, the *U.S.S. Phelps* was sent to San Francisco for refitting and, while there, it received this 48-star jack that had been produced at the Mare Island Naval Yard in November 1942.

The *U.S.S. Phelps* was awarded 12 battle stars and was the first United States warship to drop anchor in Japanese waters in World War II. This occurred at Kwajalein Island in January 1944 when, upon anchoring, this jack was raised at the ship's bow.

Flag shown flying on the U.S.S. Phelps *at the Mare Island Navy Yard, CA, 1942 is possibly the one shown above which the* Phelps *acquired during this refit.*

48-Star United States Ensign from the Invasion of Normandy on D-Day

This battle-damaged United States ensign was acquired from one of the U.S. ships involved in the Western Task Force during Operation Overlord. That was the code word for the massive Allied landings on the Normandy coast on June 6, 1944, popularly known as D-Day. The *U.S.S. Augusta* was the flagship leading the Western Task Force charged with protecting and landing the U.S. forces which stormed ashore at Utah and Omaha Beaches. Over 1,000 ships took part in the landings, but because of wartime security restraints the name of the ship that bore this flag is unknown.

This flag was donated to the Wall Street financier and promoter of Anglo-American good will, Calvin Bullock. He displayed this flag prominently at his 1 Wall Street office in New York City. There he maintained both a private collection of historic flags and the conference room of the famous Calvin Bullock Forum, a speakers' forum for renowned public figures who addressed topics of the day.

British Royal Navy White Ensign from the Invasion of Normandy on D-Day

Most Americans think of the national flag of Great Britain as combining the red cross of St. George, white cross of St. Andrew, and red cross of St. Patrick against a dark blue field. While this is the state (government) flag of Great Britain, ships registered there fly either the Red, Blue, or White Ensign. The Red and the Blue Ensigns consist of a red (or blue) field bearing the Union Jack in the hoist corner as a canton. The White Ensign is reserved for vessels of the Royal Navy. The White Ensign consists of a white field quartered by the red Cross of St. George, with the Union Jack in the upper hoist corner.

This White Ensign was flown aboard the "leading ship" of one of the assault forces to the Normandy Coast on D-Day, June 6, 1944. Two weeks later, this flag was sent as a gift to Calvin Bullock of New York City to display in his collection.

(Left)
Date:
1942
Size:
50" hoist x 88" fly
Media:
Wool bunting; cotton stars, machine sewn
Provenance:
Acquired by the Zaricor Flag Collection in 1997 from the estate of Calvin Bullock of New York City.
ZFC1072

(Right)
Date:
1944
Size:
71" hoist x 130" fly
Medium:
Wool bunting; machine-sewn
Provenance:
Acquired by the Zaricor Flag Collection in 1997 from the estate of Calvin Bullock of New York City; gifted to Calvin Bullock by Royal Navy Commander Anthony Kimmins on June 23, 1944.
ZFC0228

GALLERY VI

48-Star United States Flag Graphic

(Left)
Date:
1943
Size:
26.75" hoist x 46.375" fly
48 Stars:
July 4, 1912 – July 3, 1959 (statehood: New Mexico January 6, 1912; Arizona February 14, 1912)
Media:
Paper envelopes and paper postage stamps
Provenance:
From the collection of Kit Hinrichs.

(Inset)
Date:
1917 – 1936 (1986 reprint)
Size:
16" x 20"
Medium:
Printed paper
Provenance:
Acquired by the Zaricor Flag Collection in 1996 from the Star-Spangled Banner Flag House Collection of Baltimore, MD.
ZFC0177

This folk art flag was created at the height of World War II and is made up exclusively of stamps and envelopes of the period. Of special note are the 48 stars in the canton. Each star is created with a cancellation mark from the respective capital of the state and placed left to right, top to bottom in the order of its admission to the union. The stripes are also made up of cancelled stamps and envelopes from the original 13 colonies. Clear provenance about the graphic is scarce, but the anecdotal story asserts that it was created by an wounded Army officer who asked his men's families to mail him cancelled envelopes from each state, thus giving him the material to make a flag during his recovery.

The 48-star flag represented the nation during World War I, the Great Depression, World War II, and the beginning of the Cold War.

U.S. Navy recruiting poster

48-Star United States Flag
Home-Made in Occupied Belgium

Date:
1944

Size:
48.5" hoist x 49" fly

48 Stars:
July 4, 1912 – July 3, 1959 (statehood: New Mexico January 6, 1912; Arizona February 14, 1912)

Medium:
Cotton; hand-sewn

Provenance:
Acquired by the Zaricor Flag Collection in 1996 from the Star-Spangled Banner Flag House Collection of Baltimore, MD. ZFC0149

During the Nazi occupation of Belgium, Madame Edith Coort-Frésart and her three daughters (Marguérite-Marie, Marie-Thérèse, and Françoise) made flags from bed sheets and other materials scavenged in their household. The French Tricolor and British Union Jack were fairly easy to make while the most difficult was the Stars & Stripes. Finally, on September 7, 1944, these women—who had taken great risks in making Allied flags—were afforded the opportunity to fly them. On that day, when American and Belgian resistance forces drove the Germans out of Liège, the Coort-Frésart family responded by flying the American flag from their window. Of special note, they attempted to hang it out the window a day too early and the home received gunfire from German units still in the area.

That night an American officer, Major Arthur Tilghman Brice, stayed at their home. As a token of their thanks for the American role in the liberation of Belgium, the grateful women presented this flag to Major Brice, who took it home to Baltimore after the war. Major Brice, it turned out, was none other than the great-grandson of Francis Scott Key, who had penned the "Star Spangled Banner" in 1814.

"Service Flag"
World War II

(Right)

Date:
1942 – 1945

Size:
47.5" hoist x 67.5" fly

Media:
Wool bunting with cotton stars; machine-stitched

Provenance:
Acquired by the Zaricor Flag Collection in 1981 from Moss Landing, CA.
ZFC1019

(Inset)
Black and white photograph taken August 1, 1918. Courtesy of Motor Age.

During World War I, a special "Service Flag" for display on the "home front" was patented and widely distributed. The vertical banner, intended for display on walls, doors, or windows, consisted of a white field with a broad red border. On the white field, the home owner displaying the flag affixed as many blue, five-pointed stars, as there were household members in the armed forces. If any household member died while in the service, the household had the right to replace the blue star with a gold star. Other variations were also in vogue, but the blue and the gold stars were common to all of the regulations.

This special design has been used during World War I (1917 – 1918), World War II (1941 – 1945), the Korean War (1950 – 1952), the VietNam War (1965 – 1973), the first Gulf War (1991), and since the beginning of the War on Terrorism (2001).

Lineup of "shock troops;" volunteers who assisted farmers short of help, waiting under a Service Flag.

United States Army General Officer's Designating Flag
Lieutenant-General Matthew B. Ridgway

(Left)
Date:
1945 – 1951
Size:
35.5" hoist x 40" fly
Medium:
Rayon; machine-sewn
Provenance:
*Acquired by the Zaricor Flag Collection in 1997 from the estate of General Ridgway.
ZFC1273*

(Inset)
Cover of Life *magazine from May 12, 1952, showing General Ridgway. Courtesy of Time Life Pictures/Getty Images.*

Although the U. S. Army had long used a system of identifying commanders in the field, that system identified the command echelon of the officer without specifying his rank. By World War I, the Army had adopted an alternative system that indicated the rank of the officer flying the flag. The scheme employed was simple: using a plain red rectangular field, the general's rank insignia was applied in white in the center, with a single star representing a brigadier-general, two stars representing a major-general, three stars representing a lieutenant-general, and so on.

This flag was used by Lieutenant-General Matthew B. Ridgway from his appointment to that rank on June 4, 1945, at the close of World War II, until taking command of U. N. forces on the Korean Peninsula as a full general in April of 1951.

Franklin Delano Roosevelt was president of the United States from the beginning of its involvement in World War II until he died on April 12, 1945. When Congress designated certain individuals as 5-star generals or admirals, it became necessary to alter the presidential flag which then bore only four stars for the commander-in-chief.

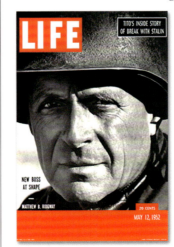

GALLERY VI

Last 48-Star United States Flag to Fly over U.S. Capitol

Date:
1959

Size:
59" hoist x 96" fly

48 Stars:
July 4, 1912 – July 3, 1959 (statehood: New Mexico January 6, 1912; Arizona February 14, 1912)

Medium:
Cotton; machine-stitched

Provenance:
Gifted to Ben Reed Zaricor in 1996 from the Star-Spangled Banner Flag House Collection of Baltimore, MD, for recovering three fragments of the original Star-Spangled Banner of 1814 that had been lost for 30 years in the museum's collection.
ZFC0179

On July 3, 1959, after 47 years of an unaltered design, the 48-star United States flag was raised over the Capitol in Washington, D.C. for the last time. After being lowered at the end of the day this very flag, the last of the old "forty-eighters," was obtained by Maryland Senator John M. Butler. He presented it to the Star-Spangled Banner Flag House Association in Baltimore.

On July 4, 1959, the 49-star flag became the official new design. Dwight D. Eisenhower was president when both the 49-star and 50-star flags were introduced.

View of a flag flying at the U.S. Capitol in Washington D.C. Photo courtesy of Jared Young, Oklahoma.

49-Star United States Flag
First to Fly Over Fort McHenry

Date:
1959

Size:
34" hoist x 57.5" fly

49 Stars:
*July 4, 1959 – July 3, 1960
(Alaska statehood
January 3, 1959)*

Medium:
Cotton; machine-sewn

Provenance:
Acquired by the Zaricor Flag Collection in 1996 from the Star-Spangled Banner Flag House Collection of Baltimore, MD.
ZFC0072

In 1959, for the first time in 47 years, the United States flag was altered. With the admission of Alaska into the Union on January 3 of that year as the 49th state, it became necessary to change the existing star pattern in the canton. President Dwight D. Eisenhower chose—from among the many designs suggested—a pattern of seven staggered rows of seven stars each. The 49-star flag became official on July 4, 1959, but was soon overtaken by events. It was to serve officially as the nation's banner for only a year because on August 21, 1959, Hawaii was admitted to the Union as the 50th state. Although its star would not become official as part of the flag until July 4, 1960, sales of the 49-star flag plummeted once Hawaiian statehood became a certainty.

To honor Alaska as "its" flag became official, a special ceremony was held at 12:05 AM on July 4, 1959 at Fort McHenry by the officials of the Star-Spangled Banner Flag House of Baltimore, MD. This particular flag was the first 49-star flag to be raised over that fort in Baltimore Harbor, and thus the first to fly officially in the country on that special day.

A SYMBOL OF WORLD POWER

World War II Allied Airman's "Chit"

After the Japanese invasion of China in the 1930s, the aviators of the American Volunteer Group adopted a patch bearing a Chinese national flag and Chinese inscription. With America's entrance into World War II, American airmen serving in the China-Burma-India theater wore a special unofficial leather or silk patch on the back of their flight jackets. These large "chits" displayed a representation of the United States flag together with the flag of the Republic of China.

Below the flags, on a white section, a message in Chinese characters explained that the airman wearing this patch was a friend of the people of China and was allied with their government against the Japanese. It went on to indicate that if the airman was discovered within Chinese lines after being shot down, he should be escorted to Republic of China forces unharmed.

Translation of Chinese: [I have] come to China to aid in the war effort [against the Japanese]. [I am] a foreigner, an American. The army and civilians form a single group. Please rescue [me]. Air Force Council.

50-Star United States Flag on an Airman's "Chit" – Vietnam War

As in World War II, when American flyers in the China-Burma-India theater had provided themselves with patches of cloth or leather called "chits," with the war in Southeast Asia, the practice was revived.

However, instead of U.S. allies' flags, the approved 1961 chit bore only the Stars & Stripes. Below this a reward text was rendered in 13 languages other than English. This particular chit was carried by an American aviator who was killed in action over Vietnam.

The American attempt to suppress the Communist-led movement to unify Vietnam as an independent nation began under President Dwight D. Eisenhower, escalating successively under Presidents John F. Kennedy, Lyndon B. Johnson, and Richard M. Nixon.

(Left)
Date:
1944 – 1945
Size:
9" x 11"
Medium:
Dyed leather, sewn
Provenance:
Acquired by the Veninga Flag Collection in 1998.
LV100 / ZFC0744

(Right)
Date:
About 1967 – 1975
Size:
9.5" x 21"
50 Stars:
Since July 4, 1960 (Hawaii statehood August 21, 1959)
Medium:
Printed cotton
Provenance:
Acquired by the Zaricor Flag Collection in 1996 from the Star-Spangled Banner Flag House Collection of Baltimore, MD.
ZFC0305

John F. Kennedy Presidential Limousine Flags, 1961–1963

Date:
*1959 – 1963
(1959 date of manufacture)*

Size:
*18" hoist x 26" fly,
exclusive of fringe*

50 Stars:
*July 4, 1960 – Present
(Hawaii statehood
August 21, 1959)*

Medium:
Bemberg rayon with machine sewn stripes and canton with Schiffli satin stitch embroidered rayon stars, rayon fringe.

Provenance:
*Acquired by the Zaricor Flag Collection in 2005 at Guernsey's, New York City; previously part of the Robert L. White Collection of the Florida International Museum, St. Petersburg, Florida; prior to that, preserved by JFK Secretary Evelyn Lincoln who acquired them from Secret Service agent/driver William Greer on November 25, 1963. Photograph courtesy of Guernsey's.
ZFC2500*

The last half of the 20th century witnessed continuing changes in the visual media which have dramatically altered our perception of history. Signal historic events were captured by amateur and professional photographers, whose images were transformed into icons of the events depicted. The assassination of President John F. Kennedy on November 22, 1963, stands paramount as the numbing event of the 1960s. The image of the presidential limousine speeding away with its pair of flags whipping wildly in the wind was seared into the nation's collective memory.

These flags, which President John F. Kennedy used throughout his 1000 days in office, were on the presidential limousine when his life was taken in Dallas. After the burial on November 25, 1963, the driver, Secret Service agent William Greer gave these flags to Mrs. Evelyn Lincoln, the late President's secretary (later private secretary to his widow, Mrs. Jacqueline Kennedy) who preserved the flags.

The U.S. presidential flag always represents an institution, not a specific person. In a monarchy the royal standard symbolizes personal hereditary rights. Our Constitution gives an individual responsibilities and rights only for so long as he serves as president. Although separate flags to designate the commander in chief of the Navy and of the Army had existed from

CONCORD & CONFLICT

1882 and 1896, a common flag for the president of the United States was not adopted until 1916.

The first president to travel with small versions of that flag and that of the United States mounted on an automobile was Woodrow Wilson in 1919. In 1945, the presidential flag was altered so as to show the stylized coat of arms of the United States surrounded by a circle of white stars equal to those on the U.S. flag. These flags were authorized for production only six days after the admission of Hawaii as the 50th state on August 21, 1959. Not only are these flags historic, but they are among the earliest examples of documented 50-star flags produced by the government.

President John F. Kennedy riding through the streets of Dallas, November 22, 1963, in presidential limousine bearing the US national flag and the presidential flag.

Date:
1961 – 1963
Size:
18" hoist x 26" fly, exclusive of fringe
50 Stars:
July 4, 1960 – Present (Hawaii statehood August 21, 1959)
Medium:
Bemberg rayon background with hand loom embroidered rayon presidential arms & stars, rayon fringe.
Provenance:
Acquired by the Zaricor Flag Collection in 2005 at Guernsey's, New York City; previously part of the Robert L. White Collection of the Florida International Museum, St. Petersburg, Florida; prior to that, preserved by JFK Secretary Evelyn Lincoln who acquired them from Secret Service agent/driver William Greer on November 25, 1963. Photograph courtesy of Guernsey's.
ZFC2501

(Inset)
Color photograph taken November 22, 1963, courtesy of Bettmann/Corbis.

50-Star United States Flag

Date:
1960

Size:
23.5" hoist x 36" fly

50 Stars:
*July 4, 1960 – Present
(Hawaii statehood
August 21, 1959)*

Medium:
Cotton blend

Provenance:
Acquired by the Veninga Flag Collection in 1999 from the family of the advisor.
ZFC0748

Detail of heading

In 1950, during the presidency of Harry S Truman, the U.S. government sent the Military Advisory Assistance Group (MAAG) to Indochina to aid the French in their colony of Vietnam. After the French withdrawal in 1954, the United States continued aid to the republic established in the southern half of the former colony.

The MAAG advisors were not to engage in combat except to defend themselves. While technically serving under the flag of the Republic of Vietnam, many of the advisors took private-purchase flags with them for unofficial display.

This very early 50-star flag was used by an advisor assigned to the MAAG in Kontum Province, Vietnam, in 1960, during the presidency of Dwight D. Eisenhower. Note the faded diagonal striations caused by hanging motionless under a fierce tropical sun.

MAAG shoulder sleeve insignia

American Peace Flag

Date:
About 1966–1971
Size:
33" hoist x 58.5" fly
Medium:
Cotton with printed peace symbol; machine-stitched
Provenance:
Acquired by the Zaricor Flag Collection in 1979 from Moss Landing, CA.
ZFC1524

During the 1950s those in Britain opposed to nuclear weapons proliferation and nuclear war began wearing a badge that integrated the international semaphore code letters N and D (for Nuclear Disarmament) within a circle. That symbol came by extension to be adopted worldwide by the "Peace Movement" of the 1960s and 1970s, for use especially but not exclusively in opposition to the Vietnam War.

The Peace Symbol was also incorporated in different ways into the United States flag, such as this popular version where it replaces the stars. Still in use today, the Peace Flag remains one of the more dramatic—and controversial—of the many variants developed over the years of the United States flag. The 3 x 5 stamp on the reverse of the flag heading indicates that it is an early peace flag, made about 1968–1971 by Paramount Flag Company of San Francisco, California.

Semaphore letters N(uclear) and D(isarmament)

50-Star United States Flag
The South Tower Flag, World Trade Center, New York, 9/11/01

Date:
Prior to 2001

Size:
30" hoist x 60" fly

50 Stars:
July 4, 1960 – Present (Hawaii statehood August 21, 1959)

Medium:
Cotton; sewn stripes and printed canton

Provenance:
Acquired by the Zaricor Flag Collection in June 2003 by private purchase. Previously displayed at the Epcot Center of Disney World, Orlando, Florida, from July 2002 through April 2003.
ZFC3911

Following 9/11, a fireman in the volunteer rescue and recovery effort asserted that he had found this flag in the rubble of the collapsed South Tower of the World Trade Center on September 18, 2001. If so, this is a rarity since very few flags were among the 9/11 artifacts retrieved. Most surviving flags went to public institutions, including the Smithsonian, the New York State Museum, and the Port Authority of New York and New Jersey. It is estimated that hundreds of flags had been in World Trade Center buildings, due both to the large number of government offices there and the American tradition of flag ownership by private individuals. Like other traumatic events in American history, 9/11 stimulated spontaneous and widespread flag display across the nation. Any flag associated with the events of 9/11 came to command great public interest when exhibited, as this one was at Disney's Epcot Center in 2002 and at The Presidio of San Francisco the following year. As a result a counterfeit version of this flag was offered for sale in 2004.

Another post-9/11 flag phenomenon was the emergence of "associated flags." Although not

50-Star United States Flag
Engine 54, Fire Department New York

From 1865 until 2001 the Fire Department of New York City saw 775 of its members die in the line of duty. On September 11, 2001, the Department lost an additional 343 firefighters, victims of the terrorist attack on the World Trade Center towers. This flag belonged to "The Pride of Mid-Town"; Battalion 9, Engine 54 and Ladder 4. This firehouse lost 15 men that day. Ladder 4 had originally been organized on September 18, 1865, while Engine 54 dates from May 26, 1884.

This flag was constantly displayed on Engine 54, in solidarity with the nation, beginning at the end of 2001. It was retired only in March 2003. During the recovery effort, rigs from this station continued to travel to the World Trade Center site in order to recover the remains of fallen brothers. Thus this flag is an important "9/11 associated flag" given its connection with the role of this Manhattan battalion following the terrorist attack. Before that tragedy, many of the rigs operated by the FDNY had routinely flown the United States flag, but since then this practice has become much more widespread.

recovered from the World Trade Center or the Pentagon, these flags have sometimes been associated with 9/11 events. Probably the most famous among them was the flag hoisted over rubble by New York City firemen who had borrowed it from a nearby yacht anchored along the Hudson River. Another flag was offered for sale on the Internet, although on 9/11 it had only been displayed at a highway construction site near the Pentagon. Public interest in authentic 9/11 flags mirrors traditional American attachment to historic flag relics in the past.

Date:
2001 – 2003

Size:
32" hoist x 60" fly

50 Stars:
July 4, 1960 – Present (Hawaii statehood August 21, 1959)

Medium:
Polyester bunting with printed stars and stripes with machine-sewn finishing

Provenance:
Acquired by the Zaricor Flag Collection in 2006 as a gift from Chief Charles Williams and Lieutenant Robert Jackson, Battalion 9, Fire Department New York.

ZFC2399

Patriotism and War

Epilogue by Henry Berger

13-Star U.S. Flag, 1795–1820

The epilogue for this volume are remarks Prof. Berger made at the Presidio in San Francisco on the occasion of the opening of the American Flag Exhibit in January 12, 2003.

Patriotic language and symbols, in the words of historian Harry Fulmer, can be drafted "into the service of manifestly unjust causes." But patriotism, like many ideas worth talking about, is a double-edged sword. Patriotism can also be—and has also been—summoned to validate, rededicate, and recommit a national community to the values and principles on which the country has been becoming established. I say "has been becoming" established because I view it as a work in progress.

The labor, the effort, the sacrifice on behalf of liberty, justice, and equality was not finished at Independence in 1776—nay, barely begun. Nor completed in 1865 with the abolition of slavery or climaxed in 1892 when the Pledge of Allegiance was written by Christian socialist Francis Bellamy, first cousin of Edward Bellamy, well-known author of the novel *Looking Backward.* Nor was the task finished in 1917 when America went to war, allegedly (and hopefully) to "make the world safe for democracy." Nor when William Tyler Page crafted the American Creed to educate the millions of immigrants who had come to America during the previous three decades—those immigrants who, among others, built the industrial capitalist order which made America by 1919 a great world power. The promise was not yet realized for workers who labored and fought for decent lives and recognition of their communal rights in the great labor struggles of the 1930s and the 1940s. Nor even finished with the accomplishments of the civil rights movements of the 1960s.

And surely not yet in our own time, when civil liberties embodied in the Constitution are being abridged—not for the first time in our history—in the name of security and when declarations of triumphalism and exceptionalism are heard in the land in the name of patriotic allegiance, when some Americans—knowing that we are the sole reigning world superpower—would display such hubris, dare we ask at this moment of crisis, in this war that we now face— may we ask with Matthew of the New Testament, "What shall it profit us if we shall gain the whole world and lose our own soul?"

The work of patriotic fulfillment as I am defining it is a continuing project. It is not static. It is not finished, nor probably will it ever be, nor should it ever be, so long as the promise of its values of freedom, justice, and equality for all is not served or is ill-served. Long ago a champion of equality, Charles Sumner of Massachusetts, reminded the country of this in an address in 1867 entitled "Are We a Nation?" at a time when the North and the South had only recently ended the carnage of civil war and were in the throes of the conflicted era of Reconstruction. He argued that the standards of patriotism to which Americans should aspire were high. Referring specifically to the flag and its stripes as the representation of patriotic virtue, he intoned: "White is for purity, red is for valor, but above all else blue is for justice. Whatever is done to advance these principles and to strengthen the Constitution as amended is patriotic. Whatever does not, diminishes and sullies the patriotic soul of the people—all the people."

A call to arms tends to distort and to simplify patriotic commitment. This was a flaw well recognized by John Quincy Adams, arguably America's greatest Secretary of State, in 1847 when the ex-President, then Congressman from Massachusetts, argued and acted against slavery and denounced what he believed was an unjust war against Mexico. Alluding to Stephen Decatur's toast in 1816—"Our country:…may she always be in the right; but our country, right or wrong"—Adams sternly replied in his contrarian fashion, "Say not thou 'my country right or wrong' nor shed thy blood for an unhallowed cause."

We live in alarming and uncertain times. The nation would be ill-served if we did not scrutinize with the utmost care that which we are ignoring at home and abroad and doing so in the name of patriotism and the flag which represents it. Many, perhaps most of us, pledge allegiance to the flag. In 1965, in the midst of the black freedom struggle of that era, novelist and essayist James Baldwin asked, "Has the flag pledged allegiance to you? To all Americans?" As you tour this fine and exquisite exhibit of American flag history you might think about that and also these words about the flag and its patriotic meaning written by Henry Ward Beecher, brother of Harriet Beecher Stowe, in another moment of patriotic crisis: "A thoughtful mind when it sees a nation's flag sees not a flag only but the nation itself and whatever may be its symbols, its insignia, one reads chiefly in the flag the government, the principles, the truths, the history, which belong to the nation that sets it forth." The history, I might suggest, is for us—for all of us—to determine and to make it good and just for us, all of us, so that about the country and its flag we can rightfully raise our voices and joyously proclaim, as Marian Anderson sang it many years ago at the Lincoln Memorial, "Of thee we sing."

Henry Berger is Emeritus Professor of History at Washington University in Saint Louis, where he taught for thirty-five years before retiring June 30, 2005. Prior to that time he was also a member of the History Department at the University of Vermont for five years. Professor Berger taught and has written about American foreign relations and about discontent, dissent, and protest in America in the Twentieth Century. He is also the editor of A William Appleman Williams Reader *(1994).*

Whose Flag Is It, Anyway?

Ben Reed Zaricor

The American flag packs emotional wallop—a potent symbol viewed passionately across our political spectrum. Much of this passion appears to be rooted in highly personalized, possessive and often misguided perceptions of "ownership."

Many people feel so strongly about "Old Glory" that they are quick to draw lines in the sand and establish their own arbitrary dictates of what constitutes "respect" and what borders on "desecration"—a term itself suggesting something with religious, symbolic power, though the American flag was the first secular national flag. When someone, or some group, violates such artificial barriers, verbal and physical blows may follow as people rush to define and defend "their" flag.

Now we are in yet another phase of America's never-ending, often heated, public debate about the flag and how it "should" be displayed and treated.

That's why actions, for example, calling for an amendment to the Constitution to prohibit "desecration" of the American flag, go to the heart of our country's sense of liberty. I simply do not understand those who want to pass laws limiting our freedom of expression, which has been guaranteed by the Constitution for over two centuries. I do not hold, as others may believe, that our flag needs protection from its people.

Many Americans may not know that, from the Colonial period to 9/11, individual Americans have created and customized the flag independent of any governmental oversight. There is, for example, a long tradition of people incorporating the flag into their clothing. Some people also have added personal elements to their flags, such as writing their names along its borders. The Sons of Liberty added a snake and "Don't Tread On Me"; centuries later, others placed the "peace symbol" in the star field to deliver a specific message in the 1960s, and again in the aftermath of 9/11, the War on Terror and the War in Iraq.

The American flag, and what it symbolizes to people around the world, mirrors our nation's history—from the struggle for independence to today's role as the global superpower. And because no single group "owns" the flag, or ever has, its design and the materials it is fashioned from illustrate the creativity, whimsy and idiosyncratic realities that are embedded in our singular culture.

Because of the powerful emotions bound up in flags, and the fascinating stories tied to them, I decided to become a collector in 1969 when many of my friends would never have dreamed of collecting such things. At that time I saw a young man in a restaurant beaten for wearing a stars and stripes vest. That experience awoke in me a passion to learn the history of our flag, which I discovered was hidden in the old flags.

The creation of a national flag center would provide a permanent, year-round venue where people could view flag exhibits and learn our country's history through these old and torn pieces of cloth. It would provide a forum for discussion of the ideas that influence our character as a nation and a place to participate in spirited educational debates and programs. Today there is no place like The Flag Center where you can see the original flags that tell so much of our country's "sea to shining sea" destiny.

Our flag tells a story of diverse ideas, cultures, personalities, races and political persuasions. It is a story both of differences and of unity. The stars on the blue canton of the flag represent individual states and their union; it is perhaps the most vivid expression of our national motto, *E Pluribus Unum*—"Out of Many, One!"

It is our flag, not the flag from our government. It is something we use in our everyday lives to express ourselves and our political freedoms. When you look at these pieces of American history, you realize they were designed, made and used by people very much like ourselves. This flag belongs to us all.

Ben Zaricor, co-sponsor of the 2003 exhibition in San Francisco, The American Flag: Two Centuries of Concord & Conflict, *began collecting flags in 1970 while a student at Washington University in St. Louis, Missouri. With his wife Louise and family, he has assembled more than 2,500 flags, quilts, and other flag related items in the Zaricor Flag Collection. A version of this essay was published in the* San Francisco Chronicle *on July 4, 2003. (Inset) Currier & Ives, 1850s (ZFC0638)*

34-Star "Grand Luminary" President Abraham Lincoln Funeral Flag, Albany, N.Y.

Date:
1861 – 1865

Size:
124" hoist x 175" fly

Media:
Wool bunting; machine-sewn with hand-sewn cotton stars

Provenance:
Acquired by Ben Zaricor from Louise Veninga, who acquired it in 1999 from James Burrus, previously in the Museum of Space and History in Hannibal, Missouri. ZFC1241

"I have often inquired of myself what great principle or idea it was that kept this Confederacy so long together. It was not the mere matter of the separation of the Colonies from the motherland; but that sentiment in the Declaration of Independence which gave liberty, not alone to the people of this country, but, I hope, to the world…But if this country cannot be saved without giving up that principle…I would rather be assassinated on this spot than surrender it…I did not expect to be called upon to say a word when I came here. I suppose it was merely to do something toward raising the flag…I have said nothing but what I am willing to live by and, if it be the pleasure of Almighty God, die by."
—*President-Elect Lincoln's address in Independence Hall, Philadelphia, Pennsylvania, February 22, 1861*

Stripes, Stars, and States

This chart shows one authentic version each for all the official and unofficial United States national flags since 1776, although it does not show every known star pattern. The top date indicates when a flag became official; the bottom date corresponds to the beginning of statehood.

Continental Colors
January 1, 1776 (Unofficial)

13-Star
June 14, 1777

States: Delaware, Pennsylvania, New Jersey, Georgia, Connecticut, Massachusetts, Maryland, South Carolina, New Hampshire, Virginia, New York, North Carolina, Rhode Island

14-Star
1791 (Unofficial)

State (Date Admitted):
Vermont (3/4/1791)

15-Star, 15-Stripe
May 1, 1795

State (Date Admitted):
Kentucky (6/1/1792)

21-Star
July 4, 1819

States (Date Admitted):
Illinois (12/3/1818)

22-Star
1819 (Unofficial)

State (Date Admitted):
Alabama (12/14/1819)

23-Star
July 4, 1820

State (Date Admitted):
Maine (3/15/1820)

24-Star
July 4, 1822

State (Date Admitted):
Missouri (8/10/1821)

30-Star
July 4, 1848

State (Date Admitted):
Wisconsin (5/29/1848)

31-Star
July 4, 1851

State (Date Admitted):
California (9/9/1850)

32-Star
July 4, 1858

State (Date Admitted):
Minnesota (5/11/1858)

33-Star
July 4, 1859

State (Date Admitted):
Oregon (2/14/1859)

39-Star
1889 (Unofficial)

State (Date Admitted):
North Dakota (11/2/1889)

40-Star
1889 (Unofficial)

State (Date Admitted):
South Dakota (11/2/1889)

41-Star
1889 (Unofficial)

State (Date Admitted):
Montana (11/8/1889)

42-Star
1889 (Unofficial)

State (Date Admitted):
Washington (11/11/1889)

48-Star
July 4, 1912

State (Date Admitted):
Arizona (2/14/1912)

49-Star
July 4, 1959

State (Date Admitted):
Alaska (1/3/1959)

50-Star
July 4, 1960

State (Date Admitted):
Hawaii (8/21/1959)

?

...and in the future?

16-Star
1796 (Unofficial)
State (Date Admitted):
Tennessee (6/1/1796)

17-Star
1803 (Unofficial)
State (Date Admitted):
Ohio (3/1/1803)

18-Star
1812 (Unofficial)
State (Date Admitted):
Louisiana (4/30/1812)

19-Star
1816 (Unofficial)
State (Date Admitted):
Indiana (12/11/1816)

20-Star
July 4, 1818
State (Date Admitted):
Mississippi (12/10/1817)

25-Star
July 4, 1836
State (Date Admitted):
Arkansas (6/15/1836)

26-Star
July 4, 1837
State (Date Admitted):
Michigan (1/26/1837)

27-Star
July 4, 1845
State (Date Admitted):
Florida (3/3/1845)

28-Star
July 4, 1846
State (Date Admitted):
Texas (12/29/1845)

29-Star
July 4, 1847
State (Date Admitted):
Iowa (12/28/1846)

34-Star
July 4, 1861
State (Date Admitted):
Kansas (1/29/1861)

35-Star
July 4, 1863
State (Date Admitted):
West Virginia (6/20/1863)

36-Star
July 4, 1865
State (Date Admitted):
Nevada (10/31/1864)

37-Star
July 4, 1867
State (Date Admitted):
Nebraska (3/1/1867)

38-Star
July 4, 1877
State (Date Admitted):
Colorado (8/1/1876)

43-Star
July 4, 1890
State (Date Admitted):
Idaho (7/3/1890)

44-Star
July 4, 1891
State (Date Admitted):
Wyoming (7/10/1890)

45-Star
July 4, 1896
State (Date Admitted):
Utah (1/4/1896)

46-Star
July 4, 1908
State (Date Admitted):
Oklahoma (11/16/1907)

47-Star
1912 (Unofficial)
State (Date Admitted):
New Mexico (1/6/1912)

Index

A
Adams, John, 11, 34
Albany (New York), 143
Alliance (ship), 21
American Anti-Slavery Society, 58
American Volunteer Group, 133
Anderson, Robert (Major, U.S. Army), 89
Andrea Doria (ship), 10
Annin & Co. (flag makers), 49, 62
Appomattox Court House (Virginia), 87, 88
Arctic, S.S. (ship), 56–57
Arthur, Chester A., 98
Associated Flags, 138–139
Augusta, U.S.S. (ship), 125

B
Baltimore (Maryland), 16, 17, 32, 33, 97, 132
Bear Flag Republic, 43
Boston (Charlestown Navy Yard), 67
Boston (Massachusetts), 10
Boston Tea Party, 11
Boxer Rebellion, 111
Bozeman Trail, 73
Bradley, Stephen R. (Senator), 30
Brice, Arthur Tilgham (Major, U.S. Army), 127
British/English flags
  Union Flag/Union Jack, 9, 10, 11, 32, 57, 110, 121, 125, 127
  Blue Ensign, 125
  Red Ensign, 57, 125
  White Ensign, 125
Buchanan, James, 62, 66, 70
Buena Vista (battle), 46, 49
Butler, Benjamin, 26, 76, 99
Butler, John M. (Senator), 131

C
California Gold Rush, 51
Cass, Lewis, 49
Cavalry standard(s), 82
Centennial Exposition (1876), 17, 23, 92, 93, 95, 99, 100
China (Republic of) flag, 133
Chit flag(s), 133
Cincinnati (Ohio), 72
Claveau (flag artist), 65
Claypoole, Elizabeth *See* Ross, Elizabeth
Cleveland, Grover, 29, 107, 108
Columbian Exposition (1893), 17
Commodore Morris, U.S.S. (ship), 23
Compromise of 1820 (Missouri Compromise), 37, 52
Compromise of 1850, 51, 52, 54, 59
Concentric Rings (star pattern)
  Single Ring, 2, 13, 17, 19, 35, 36, 47, 63
  Double Rings, 48, 49, 61, 70, 73, 83, 89, 94, 96–97, 117
  Triple Rings, 94, 106–107
Confederate States of America, National Flag "Stars & Bars," 66
Continental Colors, 10
Coolidge, Calvin, 116
Coort-Frésart (family), 127
Custer, Elizabeth (Libbie), 86–87
Custer, George Armstrong (Maj.-General, U.S. Army), 78, 79, 83, 84, 85, 86–87

D
Dallas (Texas), 134–135
Davis, Horatio (Colonel, Louisiana Militia), 45
Davis, Jefferson, 66
Davis, Samuel B., 45
D-Day (6 June 1944), 125
Declaration of Independence, 8, 9, 11, 13, 37, 46, 93, 94
Dettra Flag Company, 123

E
E Pluribus Unum (U.S. Motto), 34, 39, 98, 142
Economy flag (a.k.a. parade flag), 48, 49, 94
Eisenhower, Dwight D., 116, 131, 132, 133
English, William H., 13
Exclusionary flags, 59, 61, 63

F
Fall River (Massachusetts), 46
Farrington, D.W.C., 26
Fillmore, Millard, 54
Flag chart(s), 47
Flag derivatives, 101–102
Flag legislation
  Act of 27 March 1794, 30
  Act of 4 April 1818, 37, 38, 54, 73
  Resolution of 14 June 1777, 8
  1942 Flag Code, 25
Flowers, Benjamin (Colonel, Continental Army), 16
Forster, Samuel (Lieutenant, Essex County Militia), 9
Fort Belknap Indian Reservation, 102
Fort McHenry (Baltimore Harbor), 16, 33, 132
Fort Phil Kearney (Wyoming Territrory), 71
Fort Sumter (Charleston Harbor, S.C.), 62, 89
Frémont Flag, 13
French Tricolor, 121, 127
Fugitive Slave Act (Law), 59

G
Garfield, James A., 98
Garrison, William Lloyd, 58
General Armstrong (ship), 39
Geronimo (Indian leader), 109
Gildersleeve, S., 41
Grand Luminary (star pattern), 34, 38, 39, 40–41, 44–45, 54, 60, 90–91, 98
Grant, Ulysses S., 21, 23, 95
Great Seal of the United States, 15, 46, 55, 57, 64–65, 68, 72, 78, 117, 119
Great White Fleet, 29, 111, 112
Green, C.H., 43
Guerrière (ship), 45
Guidon(s), 78, 79, 80, 81, 83, 85, 86–87, 109, 120
Guilford Flag, 13
Greer, William, 134–135

H
Hamilton, Schuyler (author), 17
Hancock, Winfield Scott, 13
Harding, Warren G., 116
Harrison, Benjamin, 29, 98, 101, 104, 105, 107
Harrison, William Henry, 48, 53
Hayes, Dr. Isaac Israel, 61
Hayes, Rutherford B., 29, 98
Hayes Arctic Expedition, 61
Headquarters (designating) flags
  2nd Division, 9th Army Corps, 77
  2nd Brigade, 4th Division, Wilson's Cavalry Corps, 79
  3rd Division, Sheridan's Cavalry Corps, 85
  Custer's personal, 79
  Sheridan's personal, 78
  Lieutenant-General M.B. Ridgway's, 129
Hewitt, Albert, 121
Hickman Field (Hawaii), 123
Holt, John (inventor), 26, 27, 42, 99
Hoover, Herbert C., 116
Hopkinson, Francis, 14
Human flag, 113
Humanity Flag, 121

I
Indian Territory, 114

J
Jack (U.S.), 32, 56–57, 124
Jefferson, Thomas, 11, 17, 34, 35
Johnson, Andrew, 23, 94

Johnson, Lyndon B., 133
Junior Branch, Order of American Mechanics, 94

K
Kennedy, John F., 133, 134–135
Kennedy, Mrs. George (flag maker), 100
Key, Francis Scott, 16, 33, 127
Kimmins, Anthony (Captain, Royal Navy), 124, 125
Kontum Province (Vietnam), 136

L
Lawton, Henry Ware (General, U.S. Army), 109
Leutze, Emanuel (artist), 17
Lewis & Clark Expedition, 17
Liège (Belgium), 127
Liliuokalani (Queen of Hawaii), 110
Lincoln, Abraham, 23, 29, 52, 53, 60, 70, 89, 91, 143
Lincoln, Evelyn, 134–135
Loane, Jabez W. (flag maker), 73, 97, 107
Logan, "Major" William H., 102
Lowell (Massachusetts), 26
Lyon, Nathaniel (Captain, General, U.S. Army), 73

M
Madison, James., 35, 36
Mare Island Navy Yard (San Francisco), 124
Marker (flank) general guide flags, 76, 89
Marschall, Nicola (artist), 66
Masonic symbolism, 46, 94
McKinley, William, 108, 111
Military organizations
  California, "Evergreen Home Guard", 64–65
  Connecticut, 6th Regiment of Infantry, 69
  Indiana, 32nd Regiment of Infantry, 74–75
  Louisiana, 4th Regiment of Militia, 45
  Maryland, 3rd Regiment of Infantry, 47
  Massachusetts, Essex County Militia Regiment, 9
  Missouri, St. Louis Home Guard, 73
  New York (State), 1st Regiment, Veteran Engineers, 76
  Ohio, Sands' 11th Light Battery, 80
  United States Regular Army,
    11th U.S. Cavalry, 109
    18th U.S. Infantry, 71
    75th U.S. Infantry, 118–119
    308th U.S. Artillery, 120
  Divisions of the U.S. Army,
    13th Division, 119
    78th Division, 120
  Military Advisory Assistance Group, 136
Monroe, James, 36, 38
Montgomery (Alabama), 66

N
Nashville (Tennessee), 89
National standard, 68, 71, 78, 82
Navy boat flag (U.S.), 20, 22, 23, 24, 25, 26, 27, 28–29, 36, 67
New Orleans (Louisiana), 45
New York City (New York), 32, 62, 70, 75, 139
New York Fire Department,
  Battalion 9, 139
  Engine 54, 139
  Ladder 4, 139
New York (Brooklyn) Navy Yard, 29
Nixon, Richard M., 133

O
Oregon Boundary Treaty, 45
Overlord, Operation, 125

P
Parade flag
  See Economy flag
Paramount Flag Company, 137
Peace flag(s), 117, 137
Pearl Harbor (Hawaii), 123
Phelps, U.S.S. (ship), 124
Philadelphia (Pennsylvania), 16, 17, 19, 21, 46, 47, 61, 70, 81, 92, 93, 100, 117
Philadelphia Academy of Natural Sciences, 35
Pickersgill, Caroline (Purdy), 16
Pickersgill, Mary, 16
Polk, James K., 19, 43, 45, 48
Potter, Robert B. (General, U.S. Army), 77
Presidential flag, 129, 134–135

Q
Quilts, 14, 46, 55, 72, 95, 110

R
Recruiting flag(s), 74–75
Regimental color(s), 71, 118–119
Reid, Samuel C. (Privateer Captain), 34, 38, 39, 98
Reid, Mrs. Samuel C. (flag maker), 38
Ridgway, Matthew B (General, U.S. Army), 129
Roosevelt, Franklin Delano, 116, 123, 129
Roosevelt, Theodore, 108, 114
Ross, Elizabeth ("Betsy"), 16, 17

S
Saint Louis (Missouri), 73
San Francisco (California), 124, 137
Sattwell General Hospital, 61
Schaefer, William D (Mayor), 97
Sebring, James E. (flag maker), 74
Sequoyah (State of), 114
Service Flag, 128
Sheridan, Philip (General, U.S. Army), 78, 79
Sons of Liberty, 10
"Spirit of '76" (Currier & Ives lithograph), 16
Star of Bethlehem (quilt pattern), 14
"Star-Spangled Banner" (music), 16
"Star-Spangled Banner" (Currier & Ives lithograph), 2, 142
Star-Spangled Banner Flag House, 132
Statue of Liberty, 99
Stedman, Charles (Surgeon, U.S. Navy), 24
Sudbury (England), 26

T
Taft, William Howard, 112, 114, 115, 116
Taylor, Zachary, 46, 48, 49, 51, 53
Texel (Netherlands), 21
Thomas, George H. (General, U.S. Army), 88
Trapunto, 111
Treaty of Paris (1783), 23
Truman, Harry S, 136
Tyler, John, 41

U
United States, S.S. (ship), 61
United States Bunting Company, 26, 99
United States Coast Guard, 30
United States flags
  13-Star, 12–13, 15, 17, 18–19, 20, 21, 22, 23, 25, 26, 27, 28–29, 47
  16-Star, 34, 35, 67
  17-Star, 36, 59
  18-Star, 60
  19-Star, 63
  20-Star, 36, 37
  21-Star, 38
  26-Star, 40–41, 42
  27-Star, 43
  28-Star, 44–45
  29-Star, 48
  30-Star, 49, 50–51, 53
  31-Star, 53, 54
  32-Star, 59, 62
  33-Star, 60, 64–65
  34-Star, 62, 72, 73
  35-Star, 70, 73, 74–75, 88
  36-Star, 89, 90–91
  37-Star, 94
  38-Star, 94, 96–97, 99
  39-Star, 95, 100
  40-Star, 101
  41-Star, 101
  42-Star, 104
  43-Star, 105
  44-Star, 106–107
  45-Star, 108
  46-Star, 114
  47-Star, 115
  48-Star, 116, 117, 121, 122–123, 125, 126, 127, 130–131
  49-Star, 132
  50-Star, 133, 134, 136, 138–139
United States Revenue Cutter Service, 13, 31

V
Van Buren, Martin, 41, 48
Vaux, William S. (and family), 35
Vinyard, S.S. (ship), 32

W
Washburn, J.S., 46
Washington (District of Columbia), 89, 131
Washington, George, 11, 16, 30, 34, 72
Washington Monument, 99
Weisgerber, C.H. (artist), 17
Wendover, Peter (Congressman), 33, 37, 39
Whipple, Wayne, 117
Willard, Archibald M. (artist), 17
Wilson, James (General, U.S. Army), 79, 85
Wilson, Woodrow, 116, 119, 135
Winchester (Virginia), 87
World Trade Center, South Tower, 138–139

Y
Young, Rebecca, 16, 17

Glossary

Boat flag
A reduced-size U.S. national flag, usually with only 16 or 13 stars, in use between 1857 and 1916 on certain U.S. Navy boats

Bunting
Strong, loosely woven material (originally always of wool) used for making flags

Canton
The area in the upper hoist corner of a flag or a rectangular field filling that area

Color
The flag of a military unit

Designating flag
The flag identifying a military headquarters during the U.S. Civil War and afterward

Economy flag
A small inexpensive flag, usually printed, for patriotic display

Ensign
A generic term for flag, especially associated with naval flags of nationality

Exclusionary Flag
A Stars & Stripes version used before 1861 by Northerners (and Southerners) in which the number of stars reflected only the free states (slave states)

Eyelet
A whipstiched heading hole, later replaced by the grommet

Field
The background of a flag

Finial
The ornament at the top of a flagstaff

Flag derivative
A non-flag artifact incorporating the symbols and/or colors of the Stars & Stripes or portions thereof

Fly
That part of a flag opposite the staff; also a synonym for the length of a flag

Grand Luminary
A Stars & Stripes of the early 19th century with a large star in the canton composed of smaller stars

Grommet
A metal ring in the heading of a flag which allows for a halyard to be attached

Guidon
A small military flag, often swallowtailed, serving as a guide to troops

Halyard/halyards
The rope by which a flag is hoisted

Heading
A piece of heavy material attached to reinforce the hoist edge of a flag

Hoist
That part of a flag nearest the staff; also a synonym for the width of a flag

Jack
A small flag flown at the prow of a vessel, usually (but not exclusively) a warship

National standard
The main U.S. regimental or battalion color of American foot troops (1787–1841), consisting of a blue field with the U.S. arms over a scroll bearing the unit name

Obverse
The side of a flag seen when its hoist or staff is to the viewer's left

Parade flag
A small flag, usually printed, intended to be carried outdoors by a marcher

Reverse
The side of a flag seen when its hoist or staff is to the viewer's right

Standard
The main regimental or battalion color of all U.S. Army mounted units, from 1808 to 1887, consisting of a blue field with the U.S. arms over a scroll bearing the unit name

Union
A distinctive flag symbol, usually appearing in the canton, indicative of the unity of two or more territories

Union Jack
A flag indicating the unity of two or more territories, used in the British and American tradition as a naval jack, fort flag, and military color

Vexillology
The scientific study of flag history, symbolism and usage